Walk DEUTERONOMY!

דברים

Words

דברים אשר דבר משה אל כל ישראל בעבר הירדן
ואתחנן אל יהוה בעת ההוא לאמר אדני יהוה
עקב תשמעון את המשפטים האלה ושמרתם
ראה אנכי נתן לפניכם היום ברכה וקללה
שפטים ושטרים תתן לך בכל שעריך
כי תצא למלחמה על איביך
כי תבוא אל הארץ
נצבים היום כלכם
וילך משה וידבר
האזינו השמים
וזאת הברכה

Jeffrey Enoch Feinberg, Ph.D.
illustrations by Kim Alan Moudy

Lederer Books
a division of
Messianic Jewish Publishers
Clarksville, Maryland

11 10 09 08 07 06   7 6 5 4 3 2

ISBN-10 1-880226-18-9
ISBN-13 978-1-880226-18-6
Library of Congress Control Number: 2003104186

Walk Deuteronomy! belongs to
the UMJC Special Collection
of recommended resources.

Messianic Jewish Publishers
P.O. Box 615
Clarksville, Maryland 21029

Distributed by
Messianic Jewish Resources International
Order line: (800) 410-7367
E-mail: lederer@messianicjewish.net
Website: www.messianicjewish.net

Acknowledgements

Special thanks to my family
and the Etz Chaim community,
who journeyed through the Torah,
week by week, year after year,
as I wrote this series.

JEF

May God open our eyes in this generation!
"ADONAI did not make this covenant with our fathers, but with us—
with us, who are all of us here alive today."
—Deuteronomy 5:3

Preface

God calls man to oversee a moral universe. The covenant spells out the relationship between man's free will and its consequences for creation. Obedience to Torah guarantees Yisra'el a path of blessing to prosperity and long life in the Promised Land. She will inherit the gates of her enemies, and finally a day will come when all the nations join with Yisra'el in singing God's praises (Dt. 32:43, Ro. 15:9–10, Gen. 22:17–18).

On the other hand, Yisra'el has free will to stray from the covenant, seek gods of other nations, and make God red-faced over her idolatry (Dt. 32:21). Instead of shaping circumstances to bless His people, God will justly punish Yisra'el, measure for measure. If Yisra'el hardens against God's judgment, she will incur a succession of curses, culminating in a DEAD end: Destruction, Exile, Assimilation, and Death as a nation. Man's descent will bring down creation, too. The Land will bear poisonous grapes, venomous vipers, blood-eating beasts, and murderous enemies (Dt. 32:32, 33, 24, 30). Under man's accursed oversight, creation will mirror these curses of God's covenant.

Sefer D'VARIM (*the Book of Words*) spells out the choice to walk in sacred covenant with God or to incur the curses. The covenant calls Yisra'el as mamlechet kohanim v'goy kadosh (*a kingdom of priests and a holy nation*). In three moving sermons, Moshe urges her to reject the lures of idolatry and then walk, hold-in-awe, obey, hearken to God's Voice, serve, and finally cleave to God (Dt. 13:4(5רד״ק)). Cleaving to God requires a holy war to purge the Land of its high places and immorality. In this way, Yisra'el shall honor God, whose holiness radiates through His Land and ultimately fills the earth with His glory.

But getting to this place does not come easily. The Land continues to be defiled by enemies who sacrifice the blood of their firstborns to foreign gods. Will the kingdom of carnivores rule the earth, spilling blood and trampling the weak under foot? Or will God's royal priesthood and holy nation sanctify life? How can New Covenant kohanim (*priests*) intercede for God's chesed (*covenant kindness*) to redeem the world?

To play the political game according to its rules dooms Yisra'el to continuous wounds until her strength is completely drained (Dt. 32:36). God asks of the wearisome Yisra'el, "Where are their gods, the rock in whom they trusted? Who ate the fat of their sacrifices and drank the wine of their drink offering?" (Dt. 32:37–38). Yisra'el must come to her senses and recognize that her covenant has consequences, both for the moral universe she creates for herself and also for the nations among whom she is called to champion God's glory. It *does* matter that Yisra'el sanctifies life and walks in covenant blessing!

Walk DEUTERONOMY! shows how Torah remains God's instruction to corporate Yisra'el, even today. The portion HA'AZINU (*give ear!*) explains Yisra'el's "partial hardening" to her own Messiah. Repenting this inherited prejudice can open the way for Yisra'el to shake free from reliance on diplomacy or military force. God promises that He will repay Yisra'el's enemies, but only in the day that Yisra'el holds fast to God or when all her strength is spent. In our role as New Covenant kohanim, we must plead with God to circumcise hearts (Dt. 30:6). We must cast aside petty jealousies and sibling rivalries to share in the glory when God restores Y'shurun to lead the nations.

JEF
Passover, 2003

Walk D*euteronomy*!

Each section begins with a "doodle" of a scene from the portion. Embedded in the scene, cursive Hebrew letters spell out the portion name. Next comes an entertaining synopsis in rhyme. Now on to the meat of the Word! Sub-section titles scope out the flow of the story across the Torah portion, the Haftarah, and related B'rit Chadashah readings. Finally, the phrase at the bottom of the page focuses the reader on the "key idea."

The *Hiker's Log* offers a cumulative summary of what has happened to date in the story, a hint at what lies ahead, a box capsulizing the summary, and a second box listing the people, places, and events to come.

For Hebrew lovers, *Compass Work* spells out the portion name letter by letter. Scripture supplies the context for this name, and the first verse is analyzed phrase by phrase. Related Words show how the root word gets used in everyday speech.

Starting with the Rishon, each segment of Torah is featured on its own page. The topic verse is quoted, key ideas are emphasized, and challenging discussion questions stimulate contemplation. Please note that the footer at the bottom of each page references the entire segment under discussion. It is recommended that the reader consult the Scripture before reading the commentary for each particular segment.

The name *Meanderings* suggests how our journey through Torah now turns to related "excursion side-trips" in the Haftarah (*Prophets*) and B'rit Chadashah (*New Covenant/New Testament*). The format matches that of the Torah sub-sections. Like the maftir, these pages feature a quote from the end of the passage being studied. Due to limited space, ideas are compact.

Features

For readers desiring to meditate on these passages, a number of cross-references (cf.) are provided. (***Please note:*** *Selections from the B'rit Chadashah reflect efforts to complement the annual reading cycle for the Torah and Haftarah. It is not suggested that the current selections are the only readings for a given portion.*)

The ***Oasis*** has two segments: *Talk Your Walk*, a conclusion drawn from the portion; and *Walk Your Talk*, a personal application. Remarks in ***Journey's End*** sum up all of Numbers.

Hebrew names for Torah portions, people, places, and terms of interest are sprinkled throughout the text to add cultural context to the story. The italicized English meaning generally follows in parentheses; otherwise, check the ***Glossary***. Whenever verse numbers vary, the references for the Tanakh are given in parentheses with the Hebrew תנ״ך to identify them.

To use this volume as a daily devotional, the following reading plan is suggested. Begin just after Shabbat to prepare for the next week's reading, typically listed on any Jewish calendar.

Sunday	*Hiker's Log* and *Compass Work* (overview)
Monday	*Rishon* and *Sheni* Sections of the Torah portion
Tuesday	*Shlishi* and *R'vi'i* Sections
Wednesday	*Chamishi* and *Shishi* Sections
Thursday	*Shvi'i* and *Maftir* Sections
Friday	*Meanderings* (Haftarah and B'rit Chadashah)
Saturday	*Oasis* (summary and application)

Readers with less time might browse each chapter as one might page through a magazine. The *Hiker's Log* and *Oasis* segments offer the best overview.

Table of

Contents

דברים from Moshe,
prophetic words,
after forty years
seem quite absurd:
"Go up! Take the land
of honey and curds!
Appoint godly judges!
Then go tend the herds!"

"You children with Josh
will enter the Land
and conquer C'na'an,
although you're outmanned.
Sons of Esau and Lot in the east—
let them stand.
The LORD will provide!
Follow His command!"

Walk D'VARIM!
1:1–3:22

Words

TORAH—Deuteronomy 1:1–3:22

HAFTARAH—Isaiah 1:1–27

B'RIT CHADASHAH—Acts 7:51–8:4

Words for Entry

⬅ Looking Back

B'REISHEET (*in the beginning*), God creates a perfect paradise. But man disobeys, paradise crashes, and humanity fragments. God starts over with Avraham, giving him land and family. Brothers fight, then reunite to live on through their sons.

In Egypt for 400 years, 70 SH'MOT (*names*) grow to 2,000,000 slaves. Finally, God sends Moshe to lead us out with a strong hand. Delivered from Pharaoh's house, Yisra'el marches to Sinai. There, God speaks! He covenants to dwell in our midst, and Yisra'el enters His household as a kingdom of priests and a holy nation. With heartfelt offerings, we build the Tabernacle. God floods it with His glory, and Moshe cannot see to minister!

B'REISHEET, in the beginning,
God creates Paradise,
but we fail to rest.
God begins again with Avraham
and his family of covenant faith.

And these are the SH'MOT,
names of the households of Yisra'el,
who go to Egypt to survive famine.
Our numbers grow. We're enslaved.
But God delivers us from bondage
and forms us into a nation!

vaYIKRA—and He calls us to
become holy, a kingdom of priests
with God at the heart of our camp.

We follow God's cloud,
but fear of giants leads to
forty years of wandering
B'MIDBAR, in the wilderness.

Finally, the new generation stands
ready to claim the Promised Land!
These are the D'VARIM—words
which Moshe spoke . . .

vaYIKRA ADONAI (*and the LORD called*) from the Tent of Meeting, telling Moshe to

Log

draw near with offerings. In that portable Sinai, God instructs Moshe on how Yisra'el is to walk in purity and minister as a holy priesthood.

All Yisra'el stands up to be counted B'MIDBAR (*in the wilderness of*) Sinai. God reorganizes the camp, His dwelling in the center and His cloud leading the way. We march out, but fear the giants. After decades of wandering, the old die off. Now, the new generation camps by the Jordan, ready to face the giants and claim the Promised Land.

Thus commences the fifth and final book of the Torah. In his first of three D'VARIM (*words/matters*), Moshe zeroes in on two crucial events—sending spies and encounters with nations. The text defines itself as be'er et-ha-torah ha-zot (*expounding on this Torah/instruction*, Dt. 1:5).

In D'VARIM . . .

The Key People are Moshe (*Moses*), speaking to all Yisra'el (*Israel*), and Y'hoshua (*Joshua*).

The Scene is b'ever haYarden ba-midbar ba-Aravah mol Suf bein-Paran oo-vein-Tofel v'Lavan va-Chatserot v'Di Zahav (*across the Jordan, in the wilderness on the plain opposite Suph, between Paran and Tophel, Laban, Hazeroth, and Di-Zahab*).

Main Events include Moshe's words reviewing the past: God's command to enter the Land, appointment of judges, spies and disbelief, 38 years of desert wandering, victory over Sichon and 'Og, land for tribes settling east of the Jordan, and encouragement for Y'hoshua.

Moshe's exhortations climax with a warning that the new generation must face the failures of the fathers in order to enter into the promises and inherit the Land . . .

The Trail Ahead ➡

The Path

אלה הדברים אשר דבר משה
אל כל ישראל בעבר הירדן
במדבר בערבה מול סוף
בין פארן ובין תפל
ולבן וחצרת ודי זהב

—דברים א/א

ם	י	רְ	בָ	דְ
mem sofeet	yod	reish	vet	dalet
M	EE	**Ree**	Vah	D'

letter (labels above), sound (row below)

words = **D′VARIM** = **דברים**

Work

The Legend

These (are) the <u>words</u>	*eleh ha-<u>d'varim</u>*	אֵלֶּה הַדְּבָרִים
that spoke Moses	*asher diber Moshe*	אֲשֶׁר דִּבֶּר מֹשֶׁה
to all Israel	*el-kol-Yisra'el*	אֶל־כָּל־יִשְׂרָאֵל
across the Jordan,	*b'ever haYarden*	בְּעֵבֶר הַיַּרְדֵּן
in the wilderness	*ba-midbar*	בַּמִּדְבָּר
on the plain opposite Suph,	*ba-Aravah mol Suf*	בָּעֲרָבָה מוֹל סוּף
between Paran	*bein-Paran*	בֵּין־פָּארָן
and between Tophel,	*oo-vein-Tofel*	וּבֵין־תֹּפֶל
and Laban and Hazeroth	*v'Lavan va-Chatserot*	וְלָבָן וַחֲצֵרֹת
and Di-Zahab.	*v'Di Zahav*	וְדִי זָהָב׃

—*Deuteronomy 1:1*

Related Words

to say, speak	*davar*	דָּבַר
thing, matter, something, word, saying, message	*davar*	דָּבָר
it doesn't matter, never mind, don't mention it	*ein davar*	אֵין דָּבָר
in vain, don't mention it, you're welcome	*al lo davar*	עַל לֹא דָבָר
Chronicles, history (words of the days)	*divrei ha-yamim*	דִּבְרֵי הַיָּמִים
Ten Commandments, Decalogue	*aseret ha-dibroht*	עֲשֶׂרֶת הַדִּבְּרוֹת
there's substance in it (there are legs to the thing)	*yesh raglayim la-davar*	יֵשׁ רַגְלַיִם לַדָּבָר
So be it! (as your words)	*ki-dvareicha!*	כִּדְבָרֶיךָ!

Hit the Trail!

Prophetic Words

> " These are the words Moshe spoke to all Isra'el on the far side of the Yarden River, in the desert, in the 'Aravah, across from Suf, between Pa'ran and Tofel, Lavan, Hatzerot and Di-Zahav. "
>
> —Dt. 1:1

"Eleh ha-d'varim (*these are the words*)" that Moshe spoke in Sefer D'VARIM (*Book of Deuteronomy/words*). Often summarized as three sermons, a song, and blessing, this book quotes Moshe's parting words in the last weeks of his life, between 1 Sh'vat, 2488 and 7 Adar, 2488 [in 1273 BCE, see Kantor, p. 34; NAV, Dt. 1:3].

Speaking b'ever ha-Yarden (*on the far side of the Jordan*, Dt. 1:1, 5), Moshe exhorts Yisra'el to cross over and enter her inheritance in the Promised Land. In Dt. 1:1, Moshe reviews all the stations where Yisra'el rebelled against God: the wilderness (Ex. 16:1–3), the Aravah (Num. 25:1–9), Yam Suf (Ex. 14:11), Pa'ran (Num. 13:14), Tophel and Lavan [see Onkelos citing Num. 10:12, 11:6, Ex. 16:34], Chatserot (Num. 12:1–16), and Di-Zahav (Ex. 32, golden calf).

Prophetic words for long life in the Land.

Moshe warns the new generation that, in order to enjoy long life in the Land, Yisra'el must take care not to repeat the sins of the fathers in the wilderness (Dt. 4:1).

? *Korach told Moshe and Aharon: Rav-lachem—too much for you! (Num. 16:3). Read Dt. 1:6–8. Why would God use the same words when directing them to leave Chorev? Why does Moshe remind the people of these words now?*

Blessings

> " May ADONAI, the God of your ancestors, increase
> you yet a thousandfold and bless you, as he has
> promised you! "
>
> —Deuteronomy 1:11

Heritage blessings were first command-ed to Adam, renewed in Noach, and granted to the Fathers Avraham, Yitzchak, and Ya'akov (Gen. 1:28, 9:1, 12:1–3, 13:15–16, 26:3–4, 28:4, 14). They now pass to Yisra'el as promises by Moshe's own words (Dt. 1:11).

Moshe blesses Yisra'el with the promises of God.

The tone changes dramati-cally in verse 12. Unable to bear the burdens of a quarrel-some people, Moshe appoints 131 judges per 1000 people (Dt. 1:12–18).

Nonetheless, the segment reverts to overpowering bless-ings that accrue to the thou-sandth generation. The phras-es "given before you" and "laid at your feet" punctuate the seed's destiny to inherit the Land (Fox, Dt. 1:21).

A change from plural to singular verb forms (a structural marker called *Numeruwechsel*) draws attention to the turning point in the text [Christensen, p. ci]. Verse 21 concludes with strength: R'eh! . . . Aleh! Resh! (*See! . . . Go up! Take possession!*)

? *Notice the use of "ha-d'varim/words" in Deuteronomy/ D'VARIM (Dt. 1:1, 18; 4:9, 13; 9:10; 10:2, 4; 28:14; 32:46). The term can mean "words, matters, things, commandments, events, or reasons." What does the term mean in Dt. 1:18?*

Hung Up by Sin

❝ You approached me, every one of you, and said, "Let's send men ahead of us to explore the country for us and bring back word concerning what route we should use in going up ..."❞—Deuteronomy 1:22

Bring back davar (*word*), the people demanded! Moshe recalls the spies' report on Canaanite strongholds (Dt. 1:22, cf. Num. 13–14) and the people's reaction.

> ### Sin hangs up the faith-walk for a whole generation.

Preoccupations with military strategy impinge on the community's faith-walk: "Yet in this davar (*matter*), you don't trust ADONAI your God," Moshe continues (Dt. 1:32), even though ADONAI ha-holech lifneichem ([*is*] *the One Who*

walks *before you*) [Dt. 1:33, a phrase connoting military leadership; Fox, p. 852, cf. Ex. 13:21–22].

God heard et-kol divrei-chem (*the voice of your words*) and swore that a whole generation would die in the wilderness. Moshe reminds the people that he also is hung up. God had told him, "You too will not go in there" (Dt. 1:37).

Ironically, two witnesses from the older generation, Kalev and Y'hoshua, will be able to enter (Dt. 1:36, 38). Why? Because they followed the LORD wholeheartedly!

❓ Read Dt. 1:37 (cf. Num. 14:44, 20:12). Explain the reason that God judged the older generation and swore that they would not enter the Land. Does Moshe die outside the Land because of the sins of the older generation? Explain.

Small Children to Inherit

" . . . your little ones, who you said would be taken as booty, and your children who don't yet know good from bad—they will go in there; I will give it to them, and they will have possession of it. "   *—Dt. 1:39*

Tapp'chem (*your little ones, toddlers*) will be protected by the LORD Himself. Far from being taken as lavaz (*plunder*), this entire younger generation will inherit the Land!

The children enter in faith what the fathers cannot take by force.

The rabbis place the age of accountability at twenty [Shabb. 32b; 1 QS 1:10–11, cited in Christensen, p. 32]. Those "who don't yet know good from bad" (Dt. 1:39) receive entry into the Promised Land, with a chance to renew creation and redeem a long-lost paradise. The young inherit a fallen creation, but they also gain entry to a Land denied their unbelieving fathers.

In fact, God told the older generation, "I am not there with you" (Dt. 1:42). When the people did not listen to the Voice of God and tried to take the Land by force, they were swarmed by the Amorites ka'asher ta'a-seinah ha-d'vorim (*just as bees do*, Dt. 1:44). Driven back to Kadesh (Dt. 1:46), Yisra'el had to remain there another 18–19 years.

Consider that "your children who don't yet know good from bad" (Dt. 1:39) enjoy a spiritual state similar to mankind before eating from the tree of knowledge. What continuities connect the Land with the Gan Eden of old?

Enough Circling

> ❝ *Finally* ADONAI *said to me, "You have been going around this mountain long enough! Head north, and give this order to the people: '. . . pass through the territory of your kinsmen . . .'"* ❞ —Dt. 2:2–4a

Rav-lachem (*too much for you*)! Head north! (Dt. 2:3). The rebellious, old generation has died, and finally the circling ends (cf. Num. 14:33). Now, the LORD points the youth toward the Land (cf. Dt. 1:6–8).

Sins of the fathers die with the fathers, so now the young can move on.

Esav lives in the territory to the north. God has not forgotten that Esav respected his own father. In fact, God granted Esav's sons an inalienable possession on the east side of the Yarden—land promised to Avraham (Gen. 17:7–8), but not included in the apportionment to the sons of Yisra'el (Num. 34:1–12).

Recall Ya'akov's mistrust when Esav offered to escort him through his land (Gen. 33:12–16). Now Esav's descendants fear Yisra'el's huge army in their midst (cf. Num. 22:3–4). To avoid disputes, God cautioned Yisra'el against taking a foothold in Esav's land when passing through (Dt. 2:4–5, but note Num. 20:14–21).

Next come lands assigned to Lot's sons, Ammon and Mo'av. These, also, are a y'rushah (*possession*), a God-given heritage not under the Canaanite ban (Dt. 2:9, 19).

? *Rav-lachem! Such words were spoken by Korach to Moshe and Aharon, leading to a bad outcome (Num. 16:3). Read Num. 14:29–33, cf. Dt. 2:2–4a. This time, God speaks the same words, with a redemptive outcome. Explain.*

War with C'na'an

> " ADONAI said to me, "See, I have begun handing over Sichon and his territory before you; start taking possession of his land." "
>
> —Deuteronomy 2:31

R'eh (*see*)! Another change from plural to singular signals a change in the organizational structure of Moshe's sermon.

Face the giants!

No longer will sons bear sins of fathers, walking circles and waiting for the old to die. Each person must assume the burden of his own disbelief and face the giants when God orders warfare. The Amorites are destroyed completely this time (Dt. 2:34, 3:6)!

Though Esav's family remained hostile, Yisra'el did not respond with a relentless war (Dt. 2:5). Such good will for Esav's seed contrasts sharply with the wars against Sichon and 'Og, whose sons embraced idolatry and other abominable practices [Shabb. 67b; Dt. 2:29–33, 3:1–3].

Thus, acts of the fathers must be redeemed by the sons. Otherwise, the consequences for future generations grow, even as the sons harden by mindlessly embracing the sins of their fathers. History hardens when sin festers.

? *Study Dt. 2:30. Notice that God "hardened his spirit and stiffened his heart." Recall God's dealings with Pharaoh (Ex. 9:12, 10:20, 27; 11:10; 14:4). Explain why Yisra'el would relive these experiences before entering the Land.*

Taking the Inheritance

> **" I gave Gil'ad to Machir; and to the Re'uveni and the Gadi I gave the territory from Gil'ad to the Arnon Valley, with the middle of the valley as the border, as far as the Yabok ... "** —Dt. 3:15–16a

"Y'rushah (*possession*)" describes an inheritance that one possesses by dispossessing others. Sons of Esav dispossessed Se'ir; sons of Lot dispossessed the Zamzummim (Dt. 2:19–22).

Redeem idolatrous lands!

Now the sons of R'uven and Gad dispossess the Amorite kingdom of Sichon (Dt. 2:24, 3:12), and the sons of M'nasheh dispossess the kingdom of 'Og (Dt. 3:13–14). These lands, part of Jordan and Syria today, cannot be integrated into lands across the Jordan, until the other tribes secure their inheritances (Dt. 3:20).

Meanwhile, these tribes are to settle their wives, kids, and cattle—so many cattle, rav lachem (*enough for you*, Dt. 3:19). The men send chalutsim (lit. *pioneers*, or "shock-troops" [JPS, Dt. 3:18]). These men "cross over" the Yarden to fight with their brothers, in a united calling to dispossess C'na'anim and to cleanse the Land of idolatry and cults which uncover the nakedness of the fathers (Gen. 9:22–25).

? "Jihad" describes a holy war initiated by the Voice of God. Read Dt. 2:31–36. Discuss how "holy wars" today differ from the commands given Yisra'el concerning the C'na'anim. Can there be a biblical "holy war" today?

Warfare—Led by God!

❝ *Also at that time I gave this order to Y'hoshua:*
". . . Don't be afraid of them, because ADONAI *your*
God will fight on your behalf." ❞

—*Deuteronomy 3:21–22*

In a holy war, God leads and fights for His people. No one should doubt His help at this time after witnessing the total destruction of Sichon and 'Og (Dt. 3:21, 4:3, 11:7). The Scripture continues, "So shall the LORD do to all the kingdoms into which you shall cross over" [JPS, Dt. 3:21; see also *Walk* GENESIS, p. 52].

To "cross over" and appropriate the inheritance will require boldness from the younger generation's new leader, Y'hoshua (lit. *God is salvation*). The maftir calls the people to this same boldness:

"Don't be afraid of them, because ADONAI your God will fight on your behalf" (Dt. 3:22).

God leads the holy war.

Moshe finds great encouragement in the LORD's call to action. God allows him to conquer and apportion lands east of the Yarden. Moshe begins to hope that God will show grace and allow him to enter the Land. But even his repentance with tears will not change the mind of God . . .

? *Torah reads: hu ha-nilcham la-chem (He is the One Who wages war for you, Dt. 3:22). Accordingly, Yisra'el is told, lo tira'um (you shall not fear them). Explain how war could still be fearsome, even with a manifest God going first.*

Tsiyon
to be Redeemed

Meander

> **" Tziyon will be redeemed by justice; and those in her who repent, by righteousness. "**
>
> —Isaiah 1:27

A brood of evildoers with depraved children hardened by sin (Is. 1:4), Yisra'el in Isaiah's day becomes like Sodom and Gomorrah—destroyed, children and all (Is. 1:10; cf. Dt. 32:32). Judges take bribes, and justice cannot be found for the orphan or widow (Is. 1:23).

> ## *A society that preys on the defenseless must be destroyed or cleansed.*

God must purify this sinful nation and restore just judges. Wicked judges who defer to the rich must be purged, even if chaos and destruction shake the society. God vows to cleanse Yisra'el's impurities as one uses lye to purify metals (Is. 1:25).

This Haftarah, third on the theme of affliction, culminates in judgment on Yisra'el. The reading always precedes Tish'ah b'Av (*the ninth of Av*), a fast day examining the destruction of both Temples and the suffering that follows from national exile. The sins of idolatry and sin'at chinam (*baseless hatred*) must be uprooted to reverse the causes of exile and loss of nationhood.

? *Lye eats into metal, liquifying and gassifying all impurities. Describe how purging a society of corruption is a first step in a process of restoration. At the time of purging, do the weak and innocent continue to suffer? Explain.*

> ❝ But Sha'ul set out to destroy the Messianic community . . . However, those who were scattered announced the Good News of the Word wherever they went. ❞
>
> —Acts 8:3–4

Hardening from the effects of sin across generations leads to Stephen's charge: "Stiff-necked people, with uncircumcised hearts and ears! You continually oppose the Ruach haKodesh! You do the same things your fathers did!" (Ac. 7:51).

Rav Sha'ul witnesses Stephen's martyrdom and looks on approvingly (Ac. 8:1). Even Stephen's last words, "Lord! Don't hold this sin against them!" (Ac. 7:60), fail to alter Sha'ul's stance. In fact, Sha'ul begins persecuting the entire Messianic Community, imprisoning men and women alike (Ac. 8:3).

God's rage at idolaters becomes Sha'ul's rage at believers in Yeshua.

The overall effect, however, scatters the community who then "announced the Good News of the Word wherever they went" (Ac. 8:4). In this way, persecution aids the spread of the Good News, much to the dismay and rage of those who see Messianic Judaism as an idolatry that must be destroyed.

? Read Dt. 32:21. First the Messianic Community is persecuted, later it is cut off from Yisra'el—made a no-people, as the goyim. Yisra'el rages all the more when believers stay cheerful and suffer for the Good News. Explain.

Talk Your Walk . . .

Torah asks, "Eichah (*How? . . .*)," a characteristic opening in a funeral dirge. So Moshe bemoans *how* he, by himself, can bear two million people, "burdensome, bothersome and quarrelsome!" (Dt. 1:12). Moshe appoints more than ten percent of the men to serve as judges (Dt. 1:15–18). He instructs these judges to pursue justice and not show favoritism. If a davar (*case*) is too difficult, Moshe himself will hear it.

The Haftarah addresses the progress of this ideal. Centuries pass. God chooses to glorify Himself in Y'rushalayim. But the city becomes corrupt, and Yesha'yahu (*Isaiah*) asks, "Eichah (*How? . . .*) the faithful city has become a whore! Once she was filled with justice, righteousness lodged in her; but now murderers!" (Is.

> *Purging sins is a painful process.*

1:21). God will redeem Tziyon "by justice, and those in her who repent, by righteousness" (Is. 1:27).

The B'rit Chadashah reverses the burden. Rav Sha'ul, blinded with rage, persecutes the Messianic Community with all the zeal of a prophet of God. But by trying in the flesh to imprison believers, Sha'ul thinks he's saving his people from idolatry. Ironically, his desperate efforts to purge only serve to spread the Good News to the four corners of the earth. What Sha'ul meant for evil, God redeems for His glory!

Oasis

. . . Walk Your Talk

Prophetic words, like cataract surgery, can cut deeply in order to effect healing. But without this cleansing power, sin hardens, bringing blindness in its wake. "Don't confuse me with the facts—my mind's made up!" Could someone say this about you? "No one is as blind as the one who will not see!" Have you thought this about someone else?

The effects of sin accumulate with time. The process is subtle. Ask someone who wears glasses, and he will tell you that loss of vision happens so gradually that its effects can creep in unnoticed for a period of months or years! In like manner, the blinding effects of sin cross over to new generations in the most subtle of ways. The sins of the fathers are inherited as easily as one's last name.

Yet you know who "pushes your buttons." You know the kinds of things you can't tolerate. More likely than not, what you really can't stand is that you have the same problem and the "button-pusher" is too close for comfort. Open your eyes and see! Rav Sha'ul saw Yeshua

> *Face it!*
> *It can hurt to heal.*

and then spent the rest of his days repenting. What are you doing now that you will need to repent later?

Shabbat Shalom!

"ואתחנן!"
Moshe pleaded
to enter the Land.
(He *thought* he was needed.)
But God said, "Enough!
SAY NO MORE!
You'll die outside
of the Land you adore."

"Climb up Mount Nebo
to gaze from afar.
Anoint Y'hoshua,
the rising star!
Warn the next generation
to follow TORAH.
You may have the blues, Mo,
but sing the Sh'ma!"

Walk VA'ET'CHANAN!
3:23–7:11

And I pleaded

TORAH—Deuteronomy 3:23–7:11
- 1st Pleading for Entry—Deuteronomy 3:23–24a
- 2nd Commandments for Entry—Deuteronomy 4:5
- 3rd Leading by Example—Deuteronomy 4:41–42
- 4th Hearing the Ten Words—Deuteronomy 5:1
- 5th Spoken by God—Deuteronomy 5:22(19 תשׁ׳׳ך)
- 6th Take it to Heart—Deuteronomy 6:4–5
- 7th Clearing the Way—Deuteronomy 7:1
- Maftir So Keep the Commands!—Deuteronomy 7:11

HAFTARAH—Isaiah 40:1–26
> Comforting Y'rushalayim—Isaiah 40:1

B'RIT CHADASHAH—Matthew 23:31–39
> Mashiach Shall Return—Matthew 23:39

Pleading Gets You Nowhere!

← Looking Back

B'REISHEET (*in the beginning*) God creates paradise, with man as the crown jewel to oversee Creation. But man disobeys, paradise crashes, and humanity fragments into nations.

Seventy SH'MOT (*names*) list Ya'akov's sons, who reunite and grow to nationhood in the bosom of Egypt, the world empire. Yisra'el grows large and suffers in slavery, until God sends Moshe to lead us out with a strong hand. At Sinai, God speaks! The nation covenants with God, who promises to dwell in our midst. Yisra'el enters God's household as a kingdom of priests, a holy nation.

VAYIKRA ADONAI (*and the LORD called*) to Moshe from His new dwelling. In that portable Sinai, God instructs Moshe on how Yisra'el is to walk in purity and minister as a holy priesthood, a light to the nations.

B'MIDBAR (*in the wilderness of*) Sinai, all Yisra'el stands up to be counted. God reorganizes the camp into a theocracy, His dwelling in the center and His cloud leading the camp. The spies' report makes us fear giants, so we wander until the old generation dies.

Across the Jordan, the new generation listens to Moshe's final **D'VARIM.** *The time has come to enter the Land of Promise!*

Says Moshe: VA'ET'CHANAN—*and I pleaded to enter myself, but I may look only from afar . . .*

In the final six weeks of his life, Moshe delivers three **D'VARIM** (*words/matters*), exhorting Yisra'el to enter the Land and appropriate her

Log

God-given heritage. These sermons give prophetic words about living with peace, security, and blessing in the Land. Moshe recounts how Yisra'el's sin hung up the last generation and resulted in the fathers dying in the wilderness, whereas the children of faith have grown to fatherhood.

Moshe exhorts the new generation to face the giants and not shrink from their calling to redeem idolatrous lands. He insists that Y'hoshua will follow God's leading to enter C'na'an and do to the Canaanites what God has done to Sichon and 'Og.

Encouraged by the miraculous victories over such awesome giants. Moshe entreats God to reconsider and allow him to enter the Land. The

In VA'ET'CHANAN . . .

The Key Person is Moshe (*Moses*), speaking to all Yisra'el (*Israel*).

The Scene is the wilderness east of the Promised Land, waiting to cross over the Yarden (*Jordan*).

Main Events include more of Moshe's words: his plea to enter the Land, God's "No," using God's ways to lead by example, warning against idolatry, honoring the LORD as God, cities of refuge, the Ten Commandments repeated for the next generation, Sh'ma Yisra'el and v'ahavta (*Hear, O Israel . . . and you shall love . . .*), and a reminder that God will be faithful to keep His covenant with those who obey.

aging leader tells Y'hoshua, Kalev, and the young generation: VA'ET'CHANAN (*and I pleaded*) with tears . . .

The Trail Ahead

The Path

וָאֶתְחַנַּ֤ן אֶל יְהֹוָה
בָּעֵ֣ת הַהִ֖וא לֵאמֹ֑ר
אֲדֹנָ֣י יְהֹוִ֗ה אַתָּ֤ה הַחִלּ֙וֹתָ֙
לְהַרְא֣וֹת אֶת עַ֫בְדְּךָ֗
אֶת גׇּדְלְךָ֗ וְאֶת יָדְךָ֖ הַחֲזָקָ֑ה

—דברים ג׳/כ״ג-כ״ד

letter:	ו	נַ	חַ	תָ	אֶ	וָ
	nun sofeet	nun	chet	tav	alef	vav
sound:	N	**Nnah**	Chah	T	(silent)-'eh	Vah

and I pleaded = VA'ET'CHANAN = וָאֶתְחַנַּ֤ן

Work

The Legend

And I pleaded	*vá-et'chanan*	וָאֶתְחַנַּן
to the LORD	*el-ADONAI*	אֶל־יְהוָה
in season that (lit. the-she),	*ba-'et ha-hee*	בָּעֵת הַהִוא
saying,	*lemor*	לֵאמֹר׃
"Lord GOD,	*Adonai ELOHIM*	אֲדֹנָי יֱהוִה
You have begun	*Atah hachilota*	אַתָּה הַחִלּוֹתָ
to show	*l'har'ot*	לְהַרְאוֹת
→ servant-Your	*et-av'd'cha*	אֶת־עַבְדְּךָ
→ greatness-Your	*et-gohd'l'cha*	אֶת־גָּדְלְךָ
and → hand-Your	*v'et-yad'cha*	וְאֶת־יָדְךָ
the strong."	*ha-chazakah*	הַחֲזָקָה

—*Deuteronomy 3:23–24a*

Related Words

be gracious, pity	*chanan*	חָנַן
beseech, implore, plead	*et'chanan*	אֶתְחַנַּן
favor, grace, beauty, charm, loveliness	*chen*	חֵן
freely, for nothing	*chinam*	חִנָּם
to find favor in the eyes of	*motse chen b'einei*	מוֹצֵא חֵן בְּעֵינֵי
The LORD God, merciful and gracious (Ex. 34:6)	*ADONAI El rachoom v'chanoon*	יְהוָה אֵל רַחוּם וְחַנּוּן

Hit the Trail!

Pleading for Entry

> **❝** *Then I pleaded with ADONAI, "Adonai ELOHIM, you have begun to reveal your greatness to your servant, and your strong hand . . ."* **❞**
>
> —*Deuteronomy 3:23–24a*

Pleading, Moshe begs for God's grace to enter the Land. Respectfully, he interlaces praise with petition: "You have begun to reveal your greatness," by vanquishing the powerful kingdoms of Sichon and 'Og (Dt. 3:24).

> *Pleas for mercy set the context for the parashah.*

But Moshe's tearful plea for mercy falls short (cf. Heb. 12:17). God replies, "Rav-lach (*Enough for you!*)" and denies Moshe his dream. He commands: al-tosef daber elai od ba-davar ha-zeh (*do not continue to speak to Me anymore about this matter*, Dt. 3:26). How ironic that God's "rav-lachem" to the younger generation commands entry (Dt. 1:6, 21), whereas His "rav-lach" to Moshe bars entry to the very same Land.

Moshe's generation did not see the Land before dying (Dt. 1:35–36); but Moshe will get to see it from afar (Dt. 3:27–28). Also, and most incredibly, God will redeem His words to Moshe. Following his death, Moshe with glorified body will awaken inside the Promised Land, next to Eliyahu and Messiah, in full view of Yeshua's closest followers (Mt. 17:1–9).

? *Read Dt. 4:4. Ha-d'veikim ba'ADONAI (those who cleave to the LORD) live to inherit the Land. Explain how the younger generation cleaved and survived. Did Moshe cleave to God in his prayers? Does God show mercy? Explain.*

Commandments for Entry

> ❝ *Look, I have taught you laws and rulings, just as* ADONAI *my God ordered me, so that you can behave accordingly in the land where you are going in order to take possession of it.* ❞ —*Deuteronomy 4:5*

R'eh (*see*)! Moshe passes on God's orders concerning conduct in the Land. Yisra'el must keep the Torah and live as a sanctified nation, a collective household of God (Dt. 4:5).

Moshe exhorts Yisra'el to remain obedient to Torah.

Nations will hear of God's laws and refer to Yisra'el as an am-chacham v'navon (*a people, wise and understanding*, Dt. 4:6). They will marvel over the wisdom of Torah (Dt. 4:8). Indeed, the passing of Torah as an everlasting heritage across generations will ensure Yisra'el both secure borders and long life in the Land (Dt. 4:9, 25, 40).

Moshe's words continue on the same theme: R'EH (*see!*) the prophetic witness of the covenant relationship, with its consequences of blessing for obedience and curses for disobedience (parashat R'EH, Dt. 11:26–16:17).

Not only does the old guard disobey and die outside the Land; Moshe himself also will die outside, as a witness to the consequences of disobedience (Dt. 4:21–22).

? • Read Dt. 4:23–28, cf. Dt. 31:18–21, Jer. 7:1–34. Remember that the First Temple is destroyed because we practice idolatry and break our side of the covenant with God. Does our covenant with God end when we break it? Explain.

Leading by Example

> **"** *Then Moshe separated three cities on the east side of the Yarden ... to which a killer might flee, that is, someone who kills by mistake ... and upon fleeing ... might live there.* **"** —Deuteronomy 4:41–42

Moshe apportions cities of refuge to the tribes settling b'ever haYarden miz'r'chah shamesh (*across the Jordan, toward the rising of the sun*, Dt. 4:41). Since God denied Moshe's plea to enter the Land, Y'hoshua will have to complete the task within C'na'an (cf. Num. 35:13–15). Moshe leads the way, designating Betser for R'uven, Ramat for Gad, and Golan for M'nasheh (Dt. 4:43).

The following verse gives us the opening words of today's hagbahah ritual, in which the Torah scroll is *ele-vated* after a public reading: "V'zot haTorah asher-sam Moshe lifnei b'nei Yisra'el" (*this is the Torah which Moses placed before the children of Israel*)" (Dt. 4:44). We follow the Torah to enter the Land!

Moshe sets the example for Y'hoshua, his successor.

The Torah service climaxes with the processional and reading of God's Word in our midst. One can almost hear God saying: Rav-lachem— *enough for you!* Enter the promises, enter the Land!

? **•** *Read Dt. 4:44–45, cf. 6:20. Jewish observances relive historical experiences. When children ask about Passover rituals, we recount the story. Explain how the Torah processional and hagbahah recount following Torah to the Land.*

Hearing the Ten Words

&& Then Moshe called to all Isra'el ... "Listen, Isra'el, to the laws and rulings which I am announcing in your hearing today, so that you will learn them and take care to obey them." && —*Deuteronomy 5:1*

S'fardim customarily hear Torah read immediately after it is elevated for hagbahah. As Moshe once climbed Sinai and repeated God's words to the people, so now Moshe assembles the people once again to hear and obey God's Word. He relives how the LORD spoke personally to all the people at Sinai, from the midst of a terrifying fire, panim b'fanim (*face in face*, Dt. 5:4–5).

Thus, this segment recalls the D'var-ADONAI (the Word of the LORD) spoken to the younger generation when all were under the age of accountability: "I am ADONAI your God, who brought you out . . . You are to have no other gods before me" (Dt. 5:6–7). In this way, every generation must hear the Torah and obey it for themselves.

God personally instructs His children.

Reflecting this memory, the liturgy service structures a d'rash (*inquiry*) after chanting of the portion. Torah must penetrate to the heart to mold habit patterns (cf. Dt. 6:6).

? *God spoke the Ten Words (Dt. 4:13); yet written accounts command, "shamor" (safeguard, Dt. 5:12) and "zachor" (remember, Ex. 20:8) Shabbat. The Mekhilta claims the people heard <u>both</u> words at the same time. Comment.*

Spoken by God

❝ These words ADONAI spoke . . . at the mountain from fire, cloud and thick mist, in a loud voice; then it ceased. But he wrote them on two stone tablets, which he gave to me. ❞ —Dt. 5:22 (19ךֹנ״ֵת)

Receiving the Ten Words at Sinai, straight from the Voice of ADONAI, terrified our people (Dt. 5:22–25(19–22ךֹנ״ֵת)). Moshe reminds us how we urged him to be our ears to God and God's Voice to us. With Moshe as our mediator, the fathers of the wilderness obligated us across all generations with the words: v'shamanu v'asinu (*we will hearken and we will do*) all God commands us through Moshe (Dt. 5:27(24ךֹנ״ֵת)).

Moshe proceeds to tell us God's response: Va-yish'ma ADONAI et-kol divreichem (*and the LORD listened to the voice of your words*, Dt. 5:28(25ךֹנ״ֵת)).

Pleased with our words, God desires heartfelt obedience from generation to generation (Dt. 5:29(26ךֹנ״ֵת)).

Keeping God's covenant, spoken at Sinai, assures long life in the Land.

So God teaches Moshe kol-ha-mitsvah, v'ha-chukim v'ha-mishpatim, asher t'lam-dem (*the whole commandment, both the statutes and the regula-tions, that you are to teach them*, Dt. 5:31(28ךֹנ״ֵת)). In turn, Moshe instructs us, our sons, and our grandsons, so we can obey and live long in the Land (Dt. 6:1–3).

? Study Dt. 5:26(23ךֹנ״ֵת), 6:1–2. Explain Yisra'el's reaction to hearing God's Voice. Why is it important to hold-in-awe the LORD? Explain the connection between keeping the covenant and being fruitful and multiplying in the Land.

Take it to Heart

❝ *Sh'mA, Yisra'el! ADONAI Eloheinu, ADONAI echaD [Hear, Isra'el! ADONAI our God, ADONAI is one]; and you are to love ADONAI your God with all your heart . . .* ❞
—*Deuteronomy 6:4–5*

Sh'ma lies at the heart of Yisra'el's confession of faith. The six words of this daily prayer (Dt. 6:4) bear graphic 'ed (עד, *witness*) to ADONAI's supremacy, when scribes enlarge the letters Ayin and Dalet at the beginning and end of this pledge.

Actions emanate from loving obedience

Thus, we tell the world that there is no pantheon of deities. God alone is the sole object of our allegiance and devotion.

שְׁמַע יִשְׂרָאֵל יְהוָה אֱלֹהֵינוּ יְהוָה אֶחָד

Yeshua quoted v'ahavta as the greatest commandment of all (Matt. 22:36–38, cf. Dt. 6:5), affirming that the bedrock of our obedience arises from a whole-hearted love for God alone. Such love is relational, like a husband's love for his wife or a father's love for his child (Hos. 3:1; 11:1). It emanates from our whole being (Dt. 4:29; 6:6).

This love is not by choice; it is commanded! While spontaneous love may seem natural, Torah labels it immature. Perfect love calls for more than spontaneity—it requires commitment.

? Read Dt. 6:6, 11:18, and Jer. 31:33(32וְנָתַתִּי); cf. Jn. 14:21 and 1 Jn. 5:2. Explain how obedience can be equated with love. Now, read Dt. 5:10 and explain how perfect love flows from gratitude and devotion (and thus, obedience).

Clearing the Way

" ADONAI *your God is going to bring you into the land you will enter in order to take possession of it, and he will expel many nations ahead of you . . . bigger and stronger than you.* " —Deuteronomy 7:1

Seven nations, "more numerous and mightier (in number) than you" God will expel from the Land, including "the Hittite, the Girgashite, the Amorite, the Canaanite, the Perrizite, the Hivvite, and the Yevusite" (Fox, Dt. 7:1). Only here does Torah list all seven nations together.

Intermarriage with idolatrous tribes living in the Land is completely forbidden [Dt. 7:3; Yev. 76a]. Each of these nations practices idolatry (Dt. 7:4). Yisra'el, set apart and now holy to the LORD, must show no mercy to idolaters.

As an am s'gulah (*treasured people*), they must destroy all sites and altars devoted to foreign gods (Dt. 7:5–6). In this way, Yisra'el maintains her covenant fidelity to God.

Chosenness does not mean favoritism.

Torah does not encourage pride in one's status as a chosen people, treasured by God. God reminds Yisra'el that He did not choose for Himself a mighty or numerous people. In fact, Yisra'el was "fewest of all peoples" (Dt. 7:7).

Read Ex. 23:24, 32–33; 34:12–16; Num. 33:50–56; Dt. 12:2–3. Why would God be completely intolerant of idolatry and its fruits? Explain why God might choose a small, insignificant people to execute His purposes.

So Keep the Commands!

> **" Therefore, you are to keep the mitzvot, laws and rulings which I am giving you today, and obey them. "**
>
> —*Deuteronomy 7:11*

God tells us: shamarta et-ha-mitsvah, v'et-ha-chukim v'et-ha-mishpatim (*you shall keep the commandment, the laws and the rulings*, Dt. 7:11). In turn, we can know Him as ha-El ha-ne'eman shomer ha-b'rit v'ha-chesed (*the faithful God, who safeguards the covenant and covenant kindness*, Dt. 7:9, cf. 32:4).

God's grace extends a thousand generations "to those who love him and observe his mitzvot" (Dt. 7:9). But l'sonav el-panav (*to the one who hates Him to his face*), God m'shalem . . . l'ha'avido (*is the One Who repays . . . by causing him to perish*, Dt. 7:10).

God does not tarry! The enemy of Yisra'el will be destroyed in his own lifetime, so long as Yisra'el keeps the commands, la'asotam (*to do them*, Dt. 7:11).

God guarantees protection to Avraham's seed.

Covenant relationship clarifies that God is ever faithful to guarantee Yisra'el's safety from her enemies. Such protection extends to the thousandth generation.

? *Review Dt. 4:39–40, 8:5–6, 11:2–8. God commands Yisra'el to meet faithfulness with faithfulness—based on a love that seeks to please God, rather than a desire that seeks to avoid punishment or receive reward. Explain.*

Comforting Y'rushalayim

Meander

❝ *"Comfort and keep comforting my people," says your God. Tell Yerushalayim . . . her guilt has been paid off, that she has received at the hand of* ADONAI *double for all her sins." ❞*   —Isaiah 40:1

This Haftarah reading always falls on Shabbat Nachamu (*the Sabbath of Consolation*), after the fast day Tish'ah b'Av (*9th of Av*). God commands the prophets to speak a message of comfort to the heart of Yisra'el, even if she is in exile with her Temple destroyed [Is. 40:2; Pesik. de Rav Kah. 16:8, in Plaut and Stern, p. 450].

So begins the first of seven Haftarot of consolation: Nachamu, nachamu ami (*comfort, comfort My people*), for her iniquity is satisfied, for she has received from the hand of the LORD double for all her sins (Is. 40:1). After double punishment, ADONAI grants double comfort.

God sends prophets to comfort His people.

Neither deed nor merit brings reward for Yisra'el. But her suffering for God's glory will be redeemed. God comes with twin strengths—as the Mighty One who rescues and as the Shepherd who feeds, gathers, carries, and gently leads His people (Is. 40:10–11).

? *Haftarah readings allude to respective Torah portions until 17 Tammuz, when historical dates take over [Plaut and Stern, p. 438]. Explain how twin curses of exile and loss of the Temple create the biggest hang-up in Jewish history.*

> **❝** *For I tell you, from now on, you will not see me again until you say, "Blessed is he who comes in the name of ADONAI."* **❞**
>
> *—Matthew 23:39*

Messiah comes to comfort His people in Y'rushalayim. But His people have substituted seven woes for seven consolations (Matt. 23:13, 15, 16, 23, 25, 27, 29). The holy Temple has become a tomb for Z'charyah, the last prophet slain in the Jewish canon of sacred history (Matt. 23:35; cf. 2 Chr. 24:22).

The Temple can no longer purify sins, because its very ground is defiled (Gen. 4:10–11; Num. 35:30, 33–34). Thus, God sends His Son to comfort His people (cf. Mt. 21:33–46).

Alas, the sins of the fathers have passed to the sons, and Yeshua is greeted by a twisted generation (Matt. 23:30–32; cf. Dt. 32:5).

> *Messiah comes twice to comfort His people.*

Yeshua would have gathered the children "as a hen gathers her chickens . . . but you refused!" (Matt. 23:37). Now the curse falls—"God is abandoning your house . . . leaving it desolate" (Mt. 23:38). But Messiah will return, when greetings fill the air!

? *At Passover and Sukkot, the priests on the walls, seeing the pilgrims from afar, would call out, "Baruch haba b'shem ADONAI (blessed is he who comes in the name of the LORD)!" Relate this greeting to Messiah's return.*

Talk Your Walk . . .

V A'ET'CHANAN (*and I pleaded*) to enter the land of promise, claimed Moshe. But God turned aside fervent prayer with the words, "Don't mention this matter to me again!" His message is loud and clear—failure to give God glory, and disobedience when called to walk in the ways of Torah, cut short the divine calling to live securely in the Land. Paradoxically, after Moshe dies, God awakens him in the presence of Messiah and Eliyahu—inside the Land!

> *God comforts, but He will not set aside His glory to expedite His purposes.*

In the Haftarah, God sends the prophets to console Yisra'el for the double punishment of losing His manifest Presence in the Temple and the fate of being exiled in foreign lands. The prophets speak tender words of comfort to Yisra'el, saying that God has the strength to return His people to the Land. He will do so when Yisra'el realizes that God alone has the might and that worship of foreign idols brings nothing!

In the B'rit Chadashah, God sends the last prophet of all, His own son! Yeshua comes to gather Y'rushalayim as a hen gathers her chicks under her wings. But Y'rushalayim refuses to cleave to her Messiah. As the old guard, led by Moshe, was cursed to die in the wilderness, so now the generation that rejects Yeshua experiences the curse of an abandoned house. Romans destroy the Temple, and the people enter an exile that lasts for forty-nine generations!

Oasis

. . . Walk Your Talk

S ometimes seeking the LORD with humility and sorrow will not bring what you request. Moshe pleaded with the LORD, but he failed to enter the Land in his lifetime. The most humble man on earth spent forty years of his life in exile from Egypt, then another forty years in exile from the Land because he failed to inspire his generation to pursue a holy war at Kadesh Barnea.

One might ask the question: what kept God from answering Moshe's prayer? Torah responds that God would not listen, because Moshe failed to lead the fathers into battle (Dt. 1:22–28, 37; 3:26, 28; 4:21–22; cf. 32:51–52). The problem passed on to the next generation. A new leader, Y'hoshua, would one day send spies again and then boldly enter the Land.

When you know enough to be faithful, you can expect to inherit important responsibilities. Often, you will be called to fill the shoes of one who has walked the same path but stopped short. You must trust God and be pre-

All of us are called to walk in radical faith.

pared, if necessary, to walk on water. Will you be the one who steps out and prays, or the one who balks and pleads in sorrow?

 **Shabbat Shalom!**

עֵקֶב your listening . . .
<u>as a result of</u> your walk . . .
because you obeyed
and never did balk . . .
if you follow God closely . . .
you won't have to gawk.
When God sends the hornets,
your enemies they'll stalk!

But if you forget God,
then God forgets you
and the Promised Land
won't go to the Jew.
Exacting obedience
brings rain to the Land,
more herds, kids, and fruitfulness,
while boundaries expand.

Walk EKEV!
7:12–11:25

As a result

TORAH—Deuteronomy 7:12–11:25
   1st Super-Obedience—Deuteronomy 7:12
   2nd Satisfaction—Deuteronomy 8:11
   3rd Unmerited Inheritance—Deuteronomy 9:4
   4th New Tablets—Deuteronomy 10:1
   5th Entering Faithfulness—Deuteronomy 10:12
   6th The Rain-Fed Life—Deuteronomy 11:10–11
   7th The Earth Is Yours—Deuteronomy 11:22–23a
   Maftir Awesome Consequences!—Deuteronomy 11:25

HAFTARAH—Isaiah 49:14–51:3
   Wasteland Redeemed—Isaiah 49:14–15

B'RIT CHADASHAH—Hebrews 11:8–13
   Promises from Afar—Hebrews 11:13

As a Result of Obedience . . .
Awesome Consequences!

Looking Back

B'REISHEET (*in the beginning*), God creates a perfect paradise with man overseeing Gan Eden. But man disobeys. God scatters him as the seventy sons of Noach, who become the seventy nations of the world.

> *The new generation listens as Moshe speaks final* **D'VARIM:** *"It's time to enter Land!"*
>
> *"***VA'ET'CHANAN**—and I pleaded to enter myself, but I may look only from afar . . ."*
>
> *"***EKEV**—as a result of your obedience, God will chase away your enemies and bless you with fruitfulness!"*

Seventy **SH'MOT** (*names*) list sons of Ya'akov, who reunite as family in the bosom of Egypt. Over time, Yisra'el is greatly blessed by God and grows rapidly to over two million. However, as prophesied, the Egyptians enslave Yisra'el. God sends Moshe to bring us out with a strong hand. After sealing a formal covenant at Sinai, God elevates Yisra'el as a kingdom of priests, and we build Him a holy dwelling.

VAYIKRA ADONAI (*and the* LORD *called*) to Moshe from the Tent of Meeting. In that portable Sinai, God instructs Moshe on walking in purity and ministering as a priesthood and a holy nation.

B'MIDBAR (*in the wilderness of*) Sinai, all Yisra'el stands up to be counted. God restructures the camp as a theocracy, with His dwelling in the center and His cloud leading the way to C'na'an. After forty years wandering, we prepare to enter the Land.

The final six weeks of his life, Moshe speaks prophetic **D'VARIM** (*words/matters*), exhorting Yisra'el to enter the

Cumulative Summary

Log

Land and appropriate her God-given heritage. Three sermons urge Yisra'el to choose to stay loyal to the covenant and be blessed with long life in the Land. Moshe recounts how Yisra'el's sin hung up the last generation and resulted in the fathers dying in the wilderness. He exhorts the children, now grown, to face the giants and not shrink from the calling the way their fathers did. He insists that Y'hoshua will follow God's leading to enter C'na'an and do to the Canaanites what God did to Sichon and 'Og.

Moshe describes how he implored God: VA'ET'CHANAN (*and I pleaded*) with tears to enter the Land with the people. But God told him, "Say no more!" Moshe warns us to stay obedient to Torah, lest we also die in exile. He apportions conquered lands in the

In EKEV . . .

The Key Person is Moshe (*Moses*), speaking to all Yisra'el (*Israel*).

The Scene is the wilderness east of the Promised Land, ready to cross over the Yarden (*Jordan*).

Main Events include more talk from Moshe: future blessings for obedience, reminders from past signs and wonders, and exhortation to follow God now; remembering the golden calf, new stone tablets, and the ark; t'fillin and mezuzah as reminders; anticipating prosperity in a rain-fed Land <u>as a result of</u> super-obedience!

east, setting an example for what Y'hoshua should do after crossing the Yarden. Moshe tells Yisra'el to take the covenant to heart, warning that chosenness does not mean favoritism. Rather, obedience to Torah matters! EKEV (*as a result of*) their exacting obedience, God will bring awesome blessings to pass . . .

The Trail Ahead

The Path

וְהָיָה עֵקֶב תִּשְׁמְעוּן
אֵת הַמִּשְׁפָּטִים הָאֵלֶּה
וּשְׁמַרְתֶּם וַעֲשִׂיתֶם אֹתָם
וְשָׁמַר יהוה אֱלֹהֶיךָ לְךָ
אֶת הַבְּרִית וְאֶת הַחֶסֶד
אֲשֶׁר נִשְׁבַּע לַאֲבֹתֶיךָ

—דברים ז/יב

ב	קֶ	עֵ
letter: vet	koof	ayin
sound: V	Keh	(silent)-**'ei**

as a result = Ekev = עֵקֶב

Work

The Legend

And it was (now it shall be)	v'hayah	וְהָיָה
as a result (of) your listening to	ekev tish'm'oon	עֵקֶב תִּשְׁמְעוּן
→ the ordinances	et ha-mish'patim	אֵת הַמִּשְׁפָּטִים
the-these (i.e. these ordinances)	ha-eleh	הָאֵלֶּה
and your keeping	oo-sh'martem	וּשְׁמַרְתֶּם
and your doing them,	va-asitem otam	וַעֲשִׂיתֶם אֹתָם
and/then will keep	v'shamar	וְשָׁמַר
the LORD God-your for you	ADONAI eloheicha l'cha	יְהֹוָה אֱלֹהֶיךָ לְךָ
→ the covenant	et-ha-b'rit	אֶת־הַבְּרִית
and → the covenant-kindness	v'et-ha-chesed	וְאֶת־הַחֶסֶד
that He swore	asher nishba	אֲשֶׁר נִשְׁבַּע
to fathers-your.	la-avoteicha	לַאֲבֹתֶיךָ׃

—Deuteronomy 7:12

Related Words

as a result, consequence (Ps. 119:33, 112); recompense, reward (Ps. 19:11(12-תֵּ)) (Note: "Results" follow "on the heels of" previous action. See entries below relating to "heel.")	ekev	עֵקֶב
heel, hoof, rear of a troop, footstep	akev	עָקֵב
deceitful, showing footprints (heel marks)	akov	עָקֹב
deceitfulness (2 Ki. 10:19)	akvah	עָקְבָה
Jacob, taking by the heel (Hos. 12:4), supplanter, heel grabber	Ya'akov	יַעֲקֹב
footprints (Ps. 77:19, Song of Sol. 1:8, Ps. 89:51), step, motion of heel (Ps. 55:6)	eek'vot	עִקְּבוֹת

Hit the Trail!

Super-Obedience

> **" Because you are listening to these rulings, keeping and obeying them, ADONAI your God will keep with you the covenant and mercy that he swore to your ancestors. "**
>
> —Deuteronomy 7:12

Ekev tish'm'un et ha-mishpatim (*as a result of your hearkening to the regulations*) . . . Yisra'el's super-obedience to the covenant will reap blessing! God will reciprocate and shamar . . . et-ha-b'rit v'et-ha-chesed (*keep . . . the covenant and covenant kindness,* Dt. 7:12).

As a result of this obedience, Yisra'el will experience nothing less than explosive fruitfulness in the Land! Baruch tih'yeh mi-kol-ha-amim (*blessed shall you be from all of the peoples,* Dt. 7:14). No household will suffer barren-ness, nor will any lack for grain, wine, oil, cattle, sheep, or wealth (Dt. 7:13–14).

> ### Super-obedience transforms the nature of the moral universe.

Super-obedience to the regulations multiplies wealth beyond belief! God's chesed (*covenant kindness*) multiplies itself everywhere! In fact, all nature goes to work serving the glory of God. Not only does disease afflict one's enemies, but also the very hornets of the Land! (Dt. 7:15–16, 21).

? Review Ex. 23:28ff., cf. Dt. 7:20. Note that expanding boundaries extend from sea to sea (Ex. 23:31, Dt. 11:22–25). Explain how fruitfulness and the Promised Land expand together ekev (*as a result of*) obedience!

Satisfaction

" Be careful not to forget ADONAI your God by not obeying his mitzvot, rulings and regulations that I am giving you today. "

—Deuteronomy 8:11

Beware, lest the snare of prosperity in the Land sidetrack you, causing you to "forget ADONAI your God by not obeying his mitzvot" (Dt. 8:11).

Do not be ensnared by the lure of prosperity.

Torah does not teach the prosperity gospel. However, the obedient nation—blessed by God—can expect to eat and be satisfied. Along the way, they shall build goodly houses and multiply herds and flocks and wealth (Dt. 8:12–13).

Yet Torah warns of the danger of prosperity: v'ram l'vavecha, v'shachachta et-ADONAI (*proud-hearted, you forget the LORD*, Dt. 8:14; cf. Dt. 32:15). Inside the Land, manna will not fall. Yisra'el will perform eleven mitzvot just to make bread—sowing, plowing, reaping, binding sheaves, threshing, winnowing, selecting, grinding, sifting, kneading, and baking [Shabb. 74b].

Temptation arises to say in one's heart, "My own power and strength of my own hand has gotten me this wealth" (Dt. 8:17). Never forget God!

? Read Dt. 8:18; cf. Dt. 32:27–28. Sometimes the heart mistakenly thinks that God has played no role in creating wealth, and man feels self-sufficient. How should one deal with a sense of satisfaction that lacks humility?

Unmerited Inheritance

> **❝** *Don't think . . . "It is to reward my righteousness that* ADONAI *has brought me in to take possession of this land." No, it is because these nations have been so wicked that* ADONAI *is driving them out . . .***❞** —Dt. 9:4

Don't think: b'tsid'kati (*in my righteous-merit*) "ADONAI has brought me in to take possession of this land" (Dt. 9:4). It is the wickedness of the Canaanites that brings about their expulsion (Dt. 9:5).

Yisra'el inherits because God promised.

Know that lo v'tsidkat'cha (*not in your righteousness*) do you merit the Land. Rather, Yisra'el should regard herself as am-k'sheh-oref (*a stiff-necked people*, Dt. 9:6). To emphasize the point, Moshe lists off a string of places where Yisra'el provoked God: Chorev; Tav'erah (*blazing*); Massah (*testing*); Kivrot ha-Ta'avah (*graves of the craving*); and finally Kadesh Barnea, where Yisra'el rebelled, didn't trust, and didn't listen to God's Voice (Dt. 9:23).

The basis for Yisra'el's inheritance in the Land rests in two factors. Most importantly, God swore to the Avot (*Fathers*) that He would give this Land to their seed (Dt. 9:27, cf. Dt. 4:31). Moreover, God does not want nations to get wrong ideas!

> **?** Read Dt. 9:28, cf. Ro. 9:11–12. God's dialogue with the nations starts with Egypt, but later expands to all nations. What is God's purpose in allowing generations to die in the wilderness? Hint: study Dt. 28:64, 30:1, 5–6.

New Tablets

❝ At that time ADONAI said to me, "Cut yourself two stone tablets like the first ones, come up to me on the mountain, and make yourself an ark of wood." ❞
—Deuteronomy 10:1

P'sol-l'cha! *Carve for yourself!* "Cut yourself two stone tablets like the first ones . . . and make yourself an ark of wood," said God to Moshe (Dt. 10:1; cf. Ex. 34:1–4). Moshe had to cut out the new tablets himself (Dt. 10:3). Rashi says it's as if God said, "You broke the first set, so you carve the second set!"

Recall that God made the first tablets; but Moshe broke them at the apostasy of the golden calf, on 17 Tammuz [Ex. 32; Rashi]. Thereafter began forty days of intercession when Moshe moved his tent out of the camp and interceded for the people. Moshe insisted that God personally go before the people, and God consented (Ex. 33:12–17).

God renews broken tablets on Yom Kippur.

This second 40-day period began on 1 Elul and culminated on Yom Kippur [Ramban], when a glowing Moshe returned with new tablets inscribed by the finger of God. It's fitting that on Yom Kippur, God showed grace (Dt.10:10).

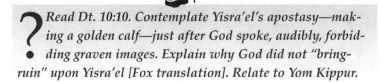

? Read Dt. 10:10. Contemplate Yisra'el's apostasy—making a golden calf—just after God spoke, audibly, forbidding graven images. Explain why God did not "bring-ruin" upon Yisra'el [Fox translation]. Relate to Yom Kippur.

Entering Faithfulness

> ❝ *So now, Isra'el, all that ADONAI your God asks from you is to fear ADONAI your God, follow all his ways, love him and serve ADONAI your God with all your heart and all your being . . .* ❞   —Dt. 10:12

God asks for ascending levels of faithfulness from His people: l'ir'ah (*to hold-in-awe*), lalechet (*to walk*) in all His ways, l'ahavah v'la'avod (*to love and to serve*); and lishmor (*to safeguard*) the Lord's commands and statutes, Dt. 10:12–13).

No one is as blind as the fathers who will not see.

But a history of rebellion takes its toll, as Yisra'el experiences certain qualities that arise from the effects of sin across generations. One can see how the old grow blind!

God commands Yisra'el to cease "stiff-necked" behaviors (Dt. 10:16b, cf. 9:6, 13, 27). He tells them: maltem et orlat l'vav'chem (*you must peel away* or *circumcise the thickening of your heart*, Dt. 10:16a). Tigay comments that this covering on the heart "renders it inaccessible to God's teaching" [p. 107].

Why must we change? Words made familiar by the Avot benediction of the Amidah (*standing prayer*) give the reason: "For ADONAI your God is God of gods and Lord of lords, ha-El, ha-Gadol, ha-Gibor, v'ha-Nora (*the great, mighty, and awesome God*)" (Dt. 10:17).

> ❓ *Read Romans 11:25–27. Notice that God will send the Kinsman Redeemer to those who await Him. The Avot prayer ends, "He will send a Redeemer to his children's children for His name's sake with love." Comment.*

The Rain-Fed Life

> **❝ For the land . . . isn't like the land of Egypt . . . the land you are crossing over to take possession of is a land of hills and valleys, which soaks up water when rain falls from the sky. ❞**   —Dt. 11:10–11

The Land Yisra'el is about to enter has a unique quality: "The eyes of ADONAI your God are always on it" (Dt. 11:12). Unlike Egypt, which is nourished by the Nile and never lacks for water, this Land is rain-fed from heaven (Dt. 11:10–11).

> *Prospering in the Land depends on loyalty and obedience to the covenant.*

But enduring in the Land is conditional. Yisra'el's survival will depend on her obedience to God; children, too, must learn this loyalty.

This segment goes on to spell out the "yoke of the commandments" [Ber. 13a]. The second paragraph, quoted after affirming the Sh'ma (Dt. 11:13–21), is inserted in the mezuzah on the doorpost and also in t'fillin (*phylacteries, prayer boxes*). Worn upon the left arm and forehead during daily morning prayer, this scripture calls to mind the covenant and its implications for long life in the Land. Everyone past bar mitzvah age must don the t'fillin and call to mind these verses that promise covenant blessing for loyalty and faithfulness (Dt. 6:8).

> **?** *Review Dt. 11:19. Rambam says, "The holiness of t'filin is great, for as long as t'filin are on the head and the arm of a man, he is humble and God-fearing" [Hil. Teph. 4]. Explain how wearing t'fillin teaches humility to the sons.*

The Earth Is Yours

**" For if you will take care to obey all these mitzvot
...to love ADONAI your God, to follow all his ways
and to cling to him, then ADONAI will expel all
these nations ahead of you ... "** —Dt. 11:22–23a

If! Ki im-shamor tish'm'run et-kol-ha-mitzvah ha-zot *(for if, keeping, you will keep all this commandment)* "to love ... to follow all his ways and to cling to him," then God will take care of driving out all the Canaanites (Dt. 11:22–23).

Cleaving to God results in super-blessings!

Complete obedience requires love, walking in God's ways, and (beyond service!) cleaving to God. The sages say that l'davkah-vo *(to cleave to Him)*, one must attach oneself to a Torah scholar [Rashi] or avoid temptations to idol worship by inspiring oneself to love God and Him alone [Ramban].

EKEV *(as a result of)* their complete obedience, God promises to greatly expand Yisra'el's boundaries. So blessed, Yisra'el will extend min-ha-midbar v'ha-l'vanon *(from the wilderness to Lebanon)* and min-ha-nahar N'har-P'rat v'ad ha-yam ha-acharon *(from the river, River Euphrates, to the last sea,* i.e. Mediterranean) (Dt. 11:24; cf. Num. 34:1–12 for less land in the east).

? *Review Gen. 22:17–18. At Moriah, God's angel promises Avraham descendants, ekev asher shamata b'koli (as a result that you listened to My Voice). Relate Avraham's obedience to blessings bestowed upon Yisra'el in Dt. 11:22–23.*

Awesome Consequences!

> ❝ No one will be able to withstand you; ADONAI your God will place the fear and dread of you on all the land you step on, as he told you. ❞
>
> —Deuteronomy 11:25

L o-yit'yatsev ish bifnei-chem (*no man will take-a-stand in your face*)! Rather, God will place "terror of you and awe of you upon all the land upon which you tread" (Fox, Dt. 11:25).

> **God blesses the nation that cleaves to Him.**

Father Avraham first trod the vast bounds of this Land, staking his claim every time he pitched his tent, during the sojournings of a lifetime. Sarah inherited the first foothold in the Land at the time of her burial. She lived a full life (120 years) and another seven (a sabbatical that extends into an everlasting inheritance in the Land).

The sages say that Messiah himself, Avraham's greatest seed, will establish the enlarged borders promised to Avraham and his seed [Gen. 15:18; Stone, p. 997, n24]. Torah promises that the nation that cleaves to God will inherit the Land. But it will be Messiah who brings the kind of obedience required to appropriate these grand promises.

Read Gen. 13:17, cf. Josh 1:3–5, 24:3, 12–13. Describe how Avraham and Y'hoshua cleaved to God and walked the lands of the expanded inheritance. Study Gen. 22:17–18. Explain how Yisra'el and the nations can inherit these lands.

> ❝ But Tziyon says, "ADONAI has abandoned me, ADONAI has forgotten me." Can a woman forget her child at the breast . . . Even if these were to forget, I would not forget you. ❞
> — Isaiah 49:14–15

Yisra'el laments that God has sent the prophets to console, but he has not come Himself! The nation feels abandoned, forgotten, and so she refuses to be comforted.

Exile does not break the covenant or signal divorce.

But God replies that exile alone does not break the covenant relationship. He asks, "Where is your mother's divorce document? . . . To which of my creditors did I sell you?" [Is. 50:1; Kimchi, Ibn Ezra, cited in Fishbane, p. 289]. Yes, God temporarily banishes Y'hudah. But as for divorce? Never! God has engraved Tsiyon on the palms of His hand, and her walls are ever before Him (Is. 49:16).

In a stunning social reversal, God prophesies that kings will tend her children (Is. 49:23). He queries, "Is my arm too short to redeem? Have I too little power to save?" (Is. 50:2). Indeed, ADONAI will comfort Tziyon, rebuild her ruins, make her desert like Eden, and bring back the days of joy and gladness! (Is. 51:3).

? *Read Is. 49:16. Explain whether or not God can forget Tsiyon. Compare and contrast the northern kingdom's divorce (Hos. 1–2; Jer. 3:1, 6–10; Ez. 16, 23) with Y'hudah's banishment until the time of reconciliation (Is. 54:4–7, 62:3–5).*

> " *All these people kept on trusting until they died, without receiving what had been promised. They had only seen it ... from a distance, while acknowledging that they were aliens ...* " —**Hebrews 11:13**

Avraham sojourned in the Land as a temporary resident, even though God had covenanted to give the Land as an everlasting heritage to his sons.

Yisra'el sees the promises from afar.

Avraham embraced the promises from afar. He purchased a cave in Chevron to bury his wife (and subsequent generations). Avraham certainly put his heels all over the Land, tenting from stop to stop, with his son and grandson, future patriarchs of the promised heritage.

Building their lives on an unseen reality guaranteed by a trustworthy God who always keeps His word, the Avot (*Fathers*) waited for the redeemed times to come.

Today, ownership of the Land is still disputed —even in places such as Chevron, the Land for which Avraham paid full price (Gen. 23:16–20). Some will say that the author of Hebrews emphasizes the transcendent hope of a heavenly city that looks beyond earthly Y'rushalayim (Heb. 11:10). Yet for that reality to transpire, even the first heaven must pass away (Rev. 21:1–3).

> **?**• *Review Dt. 11:24. Consider that the transcendent promises to Avraham include all lands along the fertile crescent from Ur to the Mediterranean Sea. Explain how Revelation 21 could look beyond a post-millennial reign.*

Talk Your Walk . . .

EKEV (*as a result of*) Yisra'el's observing the mish-patim (*regulations*) that maintain her side of the covenant, ADONAI promises to extend chesed (*covenant kindness*) that leads to super-blessings! Yisra'el can expect amazing blessings to grow out of the very first divine command to mankind—to be fruitful, multiply, fill the earth, and subdue it (Gen. 1:28, 9:1–2). The nation can expect fruitful crops, flocks, herds, and wives—resulting in vast land promises from sea to sea. Yisra'el will dispossess nations larger, stronger, and mightier than she, led by a God who fills heaven and earth with the knowledge of His glory (Dt. 11:22–25; Is. 6:3; Rev. 21:24).

> *Covenant faithfulness results in godly blessing!*

The Haftarah continues the theme of Yisra'el's failure to sow super-obedience in her covenant with the LORD. Yisra'el laments, "ADONAI has abandoned me" (Is. 49:14). But exile, loss of God's house, and temporary loss of the Land neither destroys the covenant nor divorces Yisra'el from her God. God promises to comfort Tziyon, rebuild her ruins, make her deserts like the Garden of Eden, and restore joy and gladness to earthly Y'rushalayim (Is. 51:3).

The B'rit Chadashah punctuates the theme that Avraham obeyed with zeal, tented the lands, and awaited God's promises as an alien in an alien land. In faith, he still awaits the promises seen from afar.

Conclusion

Oasis

. . . Walk Your Talk

One cannot merit either chosenness or high standing with God. Being born "right" does not assure inheritance. Esav was firstborn, yet he did not inherit the land promised to Avraham and Yitzchak. Even today, Yisra'el, the designated heir, has yet to inherit all of the Promised Land.

Yet super-blessings come ekev (*as a result of*) covenant faithfulness. For Yisra'el, walking in faithfulness hinges on service, a national obedience to the regulations of Torah. New Covenant priests must follow Yeshua's example in order to abide in His love: "If you keep my commands, you will stay in my love—just as I have kept my Father's commands and stay in his love" (John 15:10).

How will you cleave to God and obey His call on your life? After Avraham offered the ram in place of Yitzchak,

> **Perfect love cleaves to God!**

God's angel spoke from heaven, swearing that through Avraham's seed all nations could walk in blessing, ekev asher shamata b'koli (*as a result that you listened to My Voice*, Gen. 22:18). God elevates those people who put His interests above their own. ". . . you are a chosen people, the King's kohanim, a holy nation, a people for God to possess!" (1 Pet. 2:9).

 **Shabbat Shalom!**

ראה tells Yisra'el,
<u>see</u> the path—
blessings for obedience,
curses for God's wrath.
So don't bow to idols
like the pagans in Gath.
Instead do mitzvot,
stay pure, take a bath!

Walk the path of blessing,
take care of the needy.
Forgive those who owe you,
so you don't get greedy.
Go up three times to God's House.
Bring firstfruits, oh so speedy!
A fruitful day will dawn
when the Land isn't weedy!

Walk R'EH!
11:26–16:17

See!

TORAH—Deuteronomy 11:26–16:17
- 1st The Blessing and the Curse—Deuteronomy 11:26–28
- 2nd Walk the Path of Blessing—Deuteronomy 12:11
- 3rd Beware of Idolatry—Deuteronomy 12:29–30a
- 4th Be Holy to God—Deuteronomy 14:1–2a
- 5th Tithe Annually—Deuteronomy 14:22–23
- 6th Free the Debtors—Deuteronomy 15:1–2
- 7th Sanctify the Firstborns—Deuteronomy 15:19
- Maftir Pilgrimage to Y'rushalayim—Deuteronomy 16:16–17

HAFTARAH—Isaiah 54:11–55:5
- A City Unconsoled—Isaiah 54:11

B'RIT CHADASHAH—John 7:37–52
- Messiah Rejected—John 7:52

See the Path of Blessing!

← **Looking Back**

B'**REISHEET** (*in the beginning*), God creates a perfect paradise! But man disobeys, and God scatters him into the seventy nations of the world.

A list of seventy **SH'MOT** (*names*) tells of the sons of Ya'akov, whom God reunites as family. Yisra'el grows rapidly from households to nationhood. Although the Egyptians enslave us, God sends Moshe to redeem us; and He calls us to serve in His house as a kingdom of priests and a holy nation.

VAYIKRA ADONAI (*and the LORD called*) to Moshe from the newly assembled dwelling. In that portable Sinai, God instructs Moshe on house rules such as ritual purity and ministering as a priesthood.

B'MIDBAR (*in the wilderness of*) Sinai, all Yisra'el stands up to be counted. God orders the camp restructured as a theocracy. But the fathers fail to follow His lead, and God curses them to wander and die off.

Moshe's final **D'VARIM** *say it's time to enter Land!*

VA'ET'CHANAN, *Moshe pleaded, but he may only look from afar . . .*

EKEV, *as a result of, her obedience, God will bless Yisra'el!*

Moshe reminds us: **R'EH**—*see, you have a choice! Blessing and long life, or a curse with* **D***estruction,* **E***xile,* **A***ssimilation,* **D***eath.*

After forty years, Moshe exhorts the new generation to enter the Land and appropriate their God-given inheritance. Three sermons give prophetic **D'VARIM** (*words*) for long life in the Land. Moshe recounts how Yisra'el's sin resulted in the fathers dying in the wilder-

Log

ness. He exhorts the children, now grown, to face the giants and not shrink from the calling the way their fathers did.

Moshe recalls entreating God: VA'ET'CHANAN (*and I pleaded*) to enter the Land. But God answered, "Say no more!" Moshe exhorts Yisra'el to remain obedient to Torah, lest they die in exile, too. He tells us to take the covenant to heart, warning that chosenness does not mean favoritism.

Rather, obedience to Torah matters. EKEV (*as a result of*) our exacting obedience, God will bring awesome blessings to pass! Super-obedience will transform the universe, and even the hornets will chase away Yisra'el's enemies. He warns Yisra'el not to be ensnared by the lure of prosperity. Instead, success is linked to rainfall, which

In R'EH . . .

The Key Person is Moshe (*Moses*), speaking to all Yisra'el (*Israel*).

The Scene is the wilderness east of the Promised Land, ready to cross over the Yarden (*Jordan*).

Main Events include Moshe telling us to see the choice between blessing and curses; exhortation to worship God alone, in His designated place; permission to eat meat but not blood; caution against idolatry and false prophets, the imperative to destroy all high places; kosher laws, tithes, 7th year sh'mittah to cancel debts, providing for poor, freeing slaves, offering firstborn animals, and observing pilgrimage feasts of Pesach, Shavu'ot, and Sukkot.

depends solely on obedience to the covenant. R'EH (*see!*), says Moshe, two paths lie ahead. But only one path leads to long life in the Land . . .

The Trail Ahead

The Path

ראה אנכי נתן
לפניכם היום
ברכה וקללה

—דברים יא/כו

ה	אֶ	רְ
letter: hay	alef	reish
sound: H	(silent)-**'ei**	R'

see! = **R'EH** = ראה

Work

The Legend

See!	*r'eh*	רְאֵה
I	*Anochi*	אָנֹכִי
give before you all	*noten lif'neichem*	נֹתֵן לִפְנֵיכֶם
this day (lit. the day)	*ha-yom*	הַיּוֹם
(a) blessing	*b'rachah*	בְּרָכָה
and (a) curse.	*oo-k'lalah*	וּקְלָלָה׃

—Deuteronomy 11:26

Related Words

and He appeared (Gen. 18:1)	*va-yeira*	וַיֵּרָא
and I appeared (Ex. 6:3)	*va-eira*	וָאֵרָא
seer, prophetic vision	*roeh*	רֹאֶה
mirror (Job 37:18)	*r'ee*	רְאִי
vision	*ma'rah*	מַאְרָה
it seems to me	*nireh li*	נִרְאֶה לִי
see you again! (to our seeing each other)	*l'hitraot!*	לְהִתְרָאוֹת!

Hit the Trail!

The Blessing and the Curse

> ❝ See, I am setting before you today a blessing and a curse—the blessing, if you listen to the mitzvot of ADONAI . . . the curse, if you don't listen . . . but turn aside . . . and follow other gods . . . ❞ —Dt. 11:26–28

R'EH (see)! The covenant obligates the whole community to walk a path which intensifies blessings in one direction, curses in the opposite direction. Mediocrity is ruled out!

The first six verses of the parashah (Dt. 11:26–32) unfold in great detail over the next 17 chapters of Torah. In this way, the chiasm sets the stage for choosing blessings, renewing the covenant across genera-

a.	choose blessings or curses—Dt.11:26,27
b.	on Mt. Gerizim or Mt. Ebal—Dt. 11:29, 30
c.	obey chukim and mishpatim—Dt. 11: 31–32
c.	commands given—Dt. 12:1–26:16
b.	renewal at Gerizim & Ebal—Dt. 27:1–8
a.	blessings or curses...choose!—Dt. 28:1–68

God's call for covenant faithfulness takes the form of a typical Hittite Vassal treaty, with minor variations.

tions, and obeying Torah's commands in the service a redeemed nation grants her sovereign, the LORD God.

? Read Dt. 12:10. Yisra'el's constant mantra, during negotiations, can be reduced to two words: "Secure borders."
• Yet the covenant guarantees "rest from enemies" and "living in safety." Explain how Yisra'el can live in security.

Walk the Path of Blessing

" . . . then you will bring all that I am ordering you to the place ADONAI *your God chooses to have his name live . . . all your best possessions that you dedicate to* ADONAI . . . *"*   —Deuteronomy 12:11

Walking the path of blessing requires the new generation to "cross over" (*ovrim,* same root as *Ivrim/Hebrews*) the Yarden, to possess and live on the adamah (*land*).

> ### The path of blessing leads to Y'rushalayim.

The ground is accursed, and so are the sons of C'na'an (Gen. 3:17; 9:25). Yet God calls Yisra'el to redeem Creation, starting at the "place ADONAI your God chooses to have his name live" (Dt. 12:11).

As Yisra'el spreads out in the Land, travel to the central point of sacrifice will become difficult. Previously, only wild game unfit for sacrifice, such as deer and gazelles, could be slaughtered and eaten away from God's dwelling. New regulations will now allow both tahor (*ritually clean*) and tamei (*ritually impure*) to kill and eat from herds and flocks to their hearts' desire (Dt. 12:15, 20–21).

But firstfruits, firstborn domestic animals, and olot (*ascent offerings*) still must be sacrificed to ADONAI at Shiloh, and later Y'rushalayim (Lev. 7:20; cf. Dt. 12:13–16, 20–25).

> **?** Study Dt. 12:15, 20–21. Before the change of law, how could someone tamei eat meat? What ritual procedures are required for the blood of non-sacrificial animals? Does Acts 15:20 extend this requirement to gentiles? Explain.

Beware of Idolatry

> **"** *When* ADONAI *your God has cut off ahead of you the nations . . . and when you have dispossessed them . . . be careful . . . not to be trapped . . . so that you inquire after their gods . . .* **"**   —Dt. 12:29–30a

Values are caught and not taught. It is one thing to dispossess the C'na'anim and quite another to avoid being ensnared by their gods. Torah worries that Yisra'el will absorb practices that lead to the worship of Canaanite deities.

Avoid the path of curses, with its snare of idolatry.

Torah addresses various scenarios that can lure Yisra'el into idolatry: following the idolatrous prophet or religious visionary (Dt. 13:1–5(2–6תד״)),

the enticement of a relative (Dt. 13:6–11(7–12תד״)), or even the culture of an idolatrous town (Dt. 13:12–18(13–19תד״)).

Torah says to beware the one who produces a sign and also says, "Let's follow other gods, which you have not known; and let us serve them" (Dt. 13:2(3תד״)). Instead, Torah offers a solution to the snare of idolatry: telechu (*you shall walk*), tira'u (*hold-in-awe*), tish'moru (*obey*), u'v'kolo tishma'u (*and to His Voice hearken*), ta'avodu (*serve*), and finally, tid'bakun (*you shall cleave*, Dt. 13:4(5תד״)) to the LORD God.

? **•** *Torah harshly condemns Molech worship: "everything abominable . . . even their sons and their daughters they burn with fire to their gods!" (Fox, Dt. 12:31). Is today's martyrdom for Allah a path to blessing or to curses? Explain.*

Be Holy to God

> **❝** *You are the people of* ADONAI *your God. You are not to gash yourselves or shave the hair above your foreheads in mourning for the dead, because you are a people set apart as holy . . .* **❞** —Dt. 14:1–2a

As God's very own, Yisra'el must never gash herself and cause blood to flow for the dead, as the nations do (Dt. 14:1–2). Because of her covenant, Yisra'el is never totally orphaned [Abravanel].

Twice, at the start and again at the conclusion of this segment, Moshe tells Yisra'el, ki am kadosh atah l'ADONAI Eloheicha (*because you are a holy people for the* LORD *your God*, Dt. 14:2, 21).

Neither Yisra'el's mourning rites nor her eating practices should blend matters of life and death. Torah delineates ten species of kosher (*fit*) animals, four species of non-kosher animals, and 20 species of birds to avoid [Dt. 14:3–8, 11–20; Chul. 63a,b]. Predators, carnivores, and blood-eaters are eliminated from the national diet. God is God of the living and not of the dead!

Holy people must not mix life and death in matters of lifestyle.

Finally, n'veilah (*the carcass of an animal that has died of itself*) may not be eaten (Dt. 14:21). It can be given to the ger (*resident alien*) or sold to the nochri (*foreigner*).

? *Review 1 Ki. 18:28, cf. Dt. 14:21. Explain how circumcision is kosher for Yisra'el, whereas "gashing" is prohibited. Discuss whether it's a double standard to give or sell unkosher food to non-citizens.*

Tithe Annually

> **"** *Every year you must take one tenth of everything
> . . . and eat it in the presence of* ADONAI *your God.
> In the place where he chooses to have his name live
> you will eat the tenth . . .* **"**   —Dt. 14:22–23

The tithe cycle also reflects Yisra'el's covenant relationship with the Father. The first two years, the people tithe and eat firstfruits in the Presence of the LORD at the central location (Dt. 14:22–23).

> ### God commands holy fellowship.

In the third year, people remain at home and set up local atsarot (*assemblies*). They devote their ma'aser sheni (*second tithe*) to feed defenseless members of society.

This cycle repeats during years four and five, with the sixth year again being local (Dt. 14:28). The sabbatical year, no crops are sown . . . and so no tithe is given! People celebrate God's ownership of the Land, and Torah heralds sh'mittah (*release*) of all Hebrew debtors.

Christensen [p. 302] observes that local assemblies are held to feed the orphans, the widows, the poor, and the L'vi'im. Thus, society also passes on locally what God commands collectively for the nation at the central location.

> **?** *Review Dt. 14:26. People take the firstfruits rooted in the
> soil, along with firstborns from the flocks and herds, and
> heartily eat their sh'lamim (fellowship offerings) in
> God's Presence. Identify what key values Yisra'el celebrates.*

Free the Debtors

> ❝ At the end of every seven years you are to have a sh'mittah . . . every creditor is to give up what he has loaned to his fellow member . . . ADONAI's time of remission has been proclaimed. ❞   —Dt. 15:1–2

Spoken personally by the LORD at Sinai, the covenant begins, "I am ADONAI your God, who brought you out of the land of Egypt, out of the abode of slavery" (Ex. 20:2).

Sh'mittah releases all debts and debtors.

Provisions to protect the poor include: the triennial tithe (Dt. 14:22–29); remission of debts every seven years (Dt. 15:1–6); exhortation to lend to the poor (Dt. 15:7–11); and freedom for Hebrew servants (Dt. 15:12–18).

God commands sh'mittah (*release*) for those who fail to pay off debts within seven years (Dt. 15:1–6). At the time of release, servants go free— hands filled with wealth (Dt. 15:13–15; cf. Gen. 15:13–14, Ex. 12:35–36).

It is ironic that Torah offers Yisra'el a way to eliminate poverty and to lend to others as a creditor nation. Yet due to disobedience, Yisra'el will likely never attain the ideals characterizing the kind of economic freedom envisioned in God's house (Dt. 15:4, 11; cf. Mt. 26:11).

> **?** Read Dt. 15:1–2, 15. Par'oh, in Egyptian, means "Great House." How do house rules change for redeemed servants who now serve as bondservants in God's House? How does sh'mittah encourage generosity among pilgrims?

Sanctify the Firstborns

> ❝ *All the firstborn males in your herd of cattle and in your flock you are to set aside for ADONAI . . . you are not to do any work with a firstborn from your herd or shear a firstborn sheep.* ❞   —Dt. 15:19

This section links two ideas: it looks backward to the last of five provisions to protect the poor; it also looks forward as an introduction to laws regulating pilgrimage festivals.

Unblemished firstlings are holy to the LORD.

Christensen [p. 324] shows how Dt. 15:19 starts a five-part concentric cycle. The outer frame describes the consecration of firstlings (v. 19) and pouring out all blood (v. 23); the inner frame distinguishes perfect (v. 20) from blemished (v. 22) animals. The key point: blemished animals aren't fit for sacrifice (Dt. 15:21).

At seven-day festivals, Passover and Sukkot, families together with the poor and gerim (*resident aliens*) journey to offer firstfruits and eat in the Presence of the LORD. Shavu'ot, a one-day festival, requires only males to appear with firstfruits of the spring wheat.

Counting the omer begins the first seven-week cycle, between Pesach and its atseret (*restraint*) on Shavu'ot. The ancient calendar [Christensen, p. xcviii] counts three more pentecontads (50 days) before and after the seven-day festival of Sukkot.

? *Review Ex. 22:30(29 תגּ"י), which required presentation of all firstlings at the mishkan on the eighth day. Explain why the law changes, now that Yisra'el enters the Land. Relate this principal to circumcision and the sons of Yisra'el.*

Pilgrimage to Y'rushalayim

❝ *Three times a year . . . appear in the presence of* ADONAI *your God in the place which he will choose . . . every man is to give what he can, in accordance with the blessing* ADONAI *. . . has given you.* ❞ —Dt. 16:16–17

Males must appear at the central location, where God chooses to make His name to dwell, for each of three festivals: Matzah, Shavu'ot, and Sukkot. There can be no excuse for journeying up to Y'rushalayim empty-handed at the time for offering tithes and eating firstfruits (Dt. 16:16).

Harvest and feast with God in Y'rushalayim.

The maftir concludes with Sukkot. Sometimes called "the Feast" or "z'man simchateinu" *(the time of our rejoicing)*," it's the most joyous of all festivals [Tigay, p. 158; cf. Jn. 7:37–39]. At this final harvest, all of the sheva minim *(seven species: grapes, olives, dates, figs, pomegranates, wheat, and barley)* are brought to God's House as a firstfruits offering.

With sweeping promises, God blesses . . . "all your crops, and all your undertakings," so that you have "nothing but joy" (Dt. 16:15). Thus, none is to appear "empty-handed" (Dt. 16:16), and each is to give "according to the blessing God has bestowed" (Dt. 16:17).

? Read 1 Cor. 5:7 and 1 Pet. 1:17–19. In what way does Yeshua's offering fulfill Torah and generate firstfruits (1 Cor. 15:20)? Read Is. 66:20. Explain how the nations will offer Yisra'el as a minchah (grain offering/tribute).

A City Unconsoled · *Meander*

> **❝ Storm-ravaged [city], unconsoled, I will set your stones in the finest way, lay your foundations with sapphires . . .❞**
>
> —Isaiah 54:11

The prophet reports back to God that Yisra'el remains lo nuchamah (*uncomforted*, Is. 54:11). God responds tenderly, personally: v'chol-banayich limudei ADONAI, v'rav sh'lom banayich (*all your children will be taught of the LORD, and great shall be the well-being of your children*, Is. 54:13).

> ### God will send Messiah to comfort his children.

The sages say that this promise hints at the world-to-come, the days of Messiah, when the LORD is our teacher [Pes. d'Rav K. 12:22, in Plaut and Stern, p. 470].

Following the rebuilding of Tsiyon, God promises a b'rit olam (*an everlasting covenant*). Says Tigay [p. 294], "the royal covenant of David (2 Samuel 7) is now transferred to the entire people."

Yisra'el's status will change "from discomfort among the nations to being the commander over all" [Tigay, p. 292].

Whoever thirsts, whether Yisra'el or the nations, will be satisfied (Is. 55:1, 3–5).

> **?** Study John 6:44–45. Relate Yeshua's coming to God's personally coming to comfort Y'rushalayim. Read John 7:37–39, cf. Is. 55:1–3. Explain how Yeshua sought to comfort Y'rushalayim during the great pilgrimage festival.

> ❝ They replied, "You aren't from the Galil too, are you? Study the Tanakh, and see for yourself that no prophet comes from the Galil!" ❞
>
> —John 7:52

Hoshana Rabbah immediately precedes Torah's final convocation day, the day the geshem (*rain*) prayers begin. On Hoshana Rabbah, the Kohen Gadol pours out water and wine in a ritual imploring God to send the winter rains.

Yeshua comes to comfort God's city, Y'rushalayim.

Picture the worshippers encircling the Temple altar seven times, waving lulavs and chanting, "Ana ADONAI, hoshi'a na (*Please now, O LORD, save now!*)." And then silence.

The Kohen Gadol starts Simchat Beit haSho'evah (*the joy of the water drawing*) [Is. 12:3; M. Sukk. 5:1]. Suddenly, Yeshua's cry pierces the silence: "If anyone is thirsty, let him keep coming to me and drinking . . . trust in me . . . rivers of living water will flow from his inmost being!" (John 7:37–38).

Some believe. Others, hearing the Galilean accent, declare that the prophet (Dt. 18:15), born of the house of David, must come from Bethlehem, not Galilee. Thus, Yeshua's words of comfort and teaching fall on deaf ears!

? Review John 7:37–38. Standing water, from wells and cisterns, is common—warm, muddy, and often filled with spider webs and eggs. In contrast, living water is cool and vibrantly refreshing. Explain Yeshua's words of comfort.

Talk Your Walk . . .

R'EH (*see*) the path to fruitfulness, blessing, and long life in the Land! Exemplary behavior can result in miraculous blessing. However, the covenant leaves little room for mediocrity. Idolatry brings curses leading to a DEAD end, starting with *Disobedience*, then *Exile*, *Assimilation*, and *Death* as a nation.

The Haftarah picks up with the fruits of Yisra'el's idolatrous ways. Seen through the eyes of the prophet, Y'rushalayim, the place that God chooses to make His name to dwell, is left desolate, discomforted, and unconsoled. Though God sends the prophet to console his household, Y'rushalayim remains uncomforted. The prophet reports back, and so God Himself promises to lay the building stones and to personally comfort and teach His people. In fact, after Tsiyon is rebuilt, God promises a b'rit olam (*everlasting covenant*). One day Tsiyon will not thirst, for God will come to comfort her.

> **God sends His son to comfort His people.**

The B'rit Chadashah continues the thrust of the Haftarah. God sends Yeshua, understood by some as the great prophet and by others as the Messiah, the son of God. Yeshua interrupts the cries of "Hoshi'a na (*save now, please!*)" at the altar during the water-drawing ceremony on the last day of Sukkot. But alas, once again, Y'rushalayim refuses to hear and remains uncomforted!

Conclusion

Oasis

. . . Walk Your Talk

You must ask yourself, "Can I be joyous enough to give everyone a fresh start in life every seven years?" Sh'mittah (*release*) requires you to do nothing less! Perhaps a friend has taken advantage of you. Maybe a relative has borrowed so much that all you can think of is money. Maybe you feel ripped off, and maybe you have been cheated!

Now get real about life. It's one thing not to forget; it's quite another not to forgive and move on. The worst damage happens to your own disposition. If you shake with anger, then you're holding a grudge (Lev. 19:17–18). Don't fool yourself—your grudge is consuming *you*. Your greed is showing its head. As the Scripture says, ". . . sin is crouching at the door—it wants you . . ." (Gen. 4:7).

To be refreshed, you must drink your fill of living water. Joy must overflow you as it overflowed David's cup (Ps. 23:5). Choose to be consoled by Messiah and filled with His Ruach, whose fruits include joy, well-being,

> ***See!***
> ***Walk the path of blessing.***

patience, and self-control. Ask yourself: do you listen when God comforts you? See! You can be comforted, or you can let life's myriad injustices blind you.

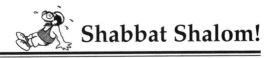 **Shabbat Shalom!**

Appoint שֹׁפְטִים—
judges at each gate.
Make a just society.
Be quick, don't wait!
Later, let the king
be chosen by God.
Priests must stay holy,
give no witch the nod.

Let justice rule
both night and day.
Give refuge in cities,
but murderers must pay.
Don't let blood
of the innocent stay—
bury the dead
without delay!

Walk SHOF'TIM!
16:18–21:9

Judges

TORAH—Deuteronomy 16:18–21:9

HAFTARAH—Isaiah 51:12–52:12

B'RIT CHADASHAH—Matthew 3:1–17

Judges for a Just Society

Hiker's

← Looking Back

B'REISHEET (*in the beginning*), God creates a perfect paradise, but man disobeys. God scatters him into seventy nations throughout the world.

When God reunites Ya'akov's sons as family, seventy SH'MOT (*names*) grow rapidly and become a threat. Par'oh [*Great House*] enslaves Yisra'el; but God, zealous for His covenant with Avraham, sends Moshe to redeem us. We shall serve in *His* house, as a kingdom of priests and a holy nation.

VAYIKRA (*and called*) the LORD to Moshe from the newly assembled mishkan (*dwelling/tent*). There, in that portable Sinai, God instructs Moshe on matters of priestly purity and ministering in His dwelling.

B'MIDBAR (*in the wilderness of*) Sinai, Yisra'el surrounds God's dwelling and starts

marching as a theocracy. The fathers fail to follow God's leading to confront the giants, and their subsequent disobedience incurs divine wrath.

Moshe speaks final **D'VARIM***: "***VA'ET'CHANAN** *to enter the Land with you, but I may only look."*

*"***EKEV** *your obedience, God will make you fruitful!* **R'EH**—*see, choose the path of blessing so you don't wind up D-E-A-D."*

"Appoint **SHOF'TIM**—*judges to set up a just society with cities of refuge. And love your neighbor as yourself."*

In Sefer **D'VARIM** (*the Book of Words*), Moshe exhorts the people to enter the Land and appropriate their God-given inheritance. Three sermons urge Yisra'el to obey so she will enjoy long life in the

Log

Land. Moshe recounts the sins of the fathers in the wilderness. He exhorts the children, now grown, to face the giants and not shrink from their calling the way their fathers did.

Moshe recalls his own sad fate: VA'ET'CHANAN (*and I pleaded*) with tears to enter the Land, but God refused. Moshe exhorts Yisra'el to remain obedient to Torah, lest they die in exile, too. He warns that chosenness does not mean favoritism.

Rather, EKEV (*as a result of*) exacting obedience, God will transform the universe and even send hornets to chase Yisra'el's enemies. He warns Yisra'el not to be ensnared by the lure of prosperity. Instead, prosperity depends solely on covenant obedience. R'EH (*see!*), two paths lie ahead. One path leads to blessings and long life

In SHOF'TIM . . .

The Key Person is Moshe (*Moses*), speaking to all Yisra'el (*Israel*).

The Scene is the wilderness east of the Promised Land, ready to cross over the Yarden (*Jordan*).

Main Events include more of Moshe's words: about appointing judges for a just society, selecting a king, Levites' inheritance, warning against pagan practices, weighing a prophet's words, cities of refuge, two witnesses needed, rules of warfare, and redeeming bloodshed.

in the Land. The other path leads to destruction, exile, assimilation, and death—a real DEAD end, with loss of sovereignty and even service to foreigners' idols!

Therefore, we must uphold God's way of life and appoint SHOF'TIM (*judges*) for a just society . . .

The Trail Ahead

The Path

שֹׁפְטִים וְשֹׁטְרִים תִּתֶּן לְךָ

בְּכָל שְׁעָרֶיךָ אֲשֶׁר יהוה אֱלֹהֶיךָ

נֹתֵן לְךָ לִשְׁבָטֶיךָ

וְשָׁפְטוּ אֶת הָעָם מִשְׁפַּט צֶדֶק

—דברים ט״ז/י״ח

	ט	פֶ	שׁ
ם	**י**		
letter: mem sofeet	yod	tet	fay	shin
sound: M	EE	**Tee**	F'	SHo

judges = SHOF'TIM = שֹׁפְטִים

Work

The Legend

Judges and officers	_shof'tim_ v'shot'rim	שֹׁפְטִים וְשֹׁטְרִים
you will give/ appoint to yourself	_titen-l'cha_	תִּתֶּן־לְךָ
in all gates-your	_b'chol-sh'areicha_	בְּכָל־שְׁעָרֶיךָ
that	_asher_	אֲשֶׁר
the LORD God-your	ADONAI Eloheicha	יְהֹוָה אֱלֹהֶיךָ
is giving to you,	_noten l'cha_	נֹתֵן לְךָ
(according) to tribes-your.	_lish'vateicha_	לִשְׁבָטֶיךָ
And they will judge	_v'shaf'too_	וְשָׁפְטוּ
→ the people	_et-ha-am_	אֶת־הָעָם
(a) judgment righteous.	_mish'pat-tsedek_	מִשְׁפַּט־צֶדֶק

—Deuteronomy 16:18

Related Words

justice, judgment, law, case, sentence; plural judgment, punishment	_mishpaht,_ _mishpatim_ _shehfet_	מִשְׁפָּט, מִשְׁפָּטִים שֶׁפֶט
judge, referee, umpire (singular, plural forms)	_shofet, shof'tim_	שׁוֹפֵט, שֹׁפְטִים
precedence (sentence of the firstling)	_mishpaht ha-b'khorah_	מִשְׁפַּט הַבְּכוֹרָה
death sentence	_mishpaht mavet_	מִשְׁפַּט מָוֶת
law court, court of justice; (also law court, court of justice)	_beit-mishpaht,_ (also _beit-din_)	בֵּית־מִשְׁפָּט, בֵּית־דִּין
jurist	_mishp'tahn_	מִשְׁפְּטָן

Hit the Trail!

The Judges

" You are to appoint judges and officers for all your gates [in the cities] ADONAI your God is giving you, tribe by tribe; and they are to judge the people with righteous judgment. " —Deuteronomy 16:18

Fundamental institutions of government include four main authority figures: shof'tim (*judges*), melech (*king*), kohanim (*priests*), and n'vi'im (*prophets*). The first segment orders the people to appoint shof'tim v'shotrim (*judges and officials*) to enforce dictates of the judiciary. Judges must pursue justice with passion (Dt. 16:20).

The judiciary consists of local courts (Dt. 16:18–20); rules and procedures to judge apostasy (Dt. 16:21–17:7); and, for complex matters, high court referral (Dt. 17:8–13).

Recall that the last segment refers to festival sacrifices (Dt. 16:13–17). Juxtaposing commands concerning the judiciary and festival sacrifices punctuates that "to do what is right and just is more pleasing to ADONAI than sacrifice" (Prov. 21:3) [Munk, p. 174].

Judges must pursue justice with passion.

What follows justice is the king (Dt. 17:14–20). Note how the Haftarah refers to Messiah as Judge, King, and Redeemer of fallen Y'rushalayim.

? Read Dt. 17:10. The precedent of haMakom Gorem (lit. the place influences the event) empowered the Sanhedrin to judge life and death, since it met near the Temple [Av. Zar. 8b]. How did exile undercut the High Court's authority?

The King

> **" When you have entered the land ADONAI your God is giving you, have taken possession of it and are living there, you may say, "I want to have a king over me . . ." "**
>
> **—Deuteronomy 17:14**

Power of the king is more limited than any other insitution [Tigay, p. 166]. In fact, Torah says nothing about the rights or authority of the king; whereas the powers, authority, and duties of the judges, priests and prophets are explicitly delineated.

Limited monarchy sets the king as first among equals.

In fact, "som tasim aleicha melech (*you may set, yes set, over you a king*)" is an optional appointment (Fox, Dt. 17:15).

The king, "one chosen by God," was appointed by a prophet, not the people (Dt. 17:15; note that Sha'ul, David, Yarov'am, and Yehu were all chosen in this way, cf. 1 Sam. 9:16–17, 10:20–24, 16:1–13; 1 Ki. 11:29–39, 2 Ki. 9:1–13).

Besides limiting the king's freedom to accumulate horses, wives, and wealth, Torah puts a most unusual requirement on the king that he must make a copy of the Torah and study it (Dt. 17:18). No other nation on earth required such scholarly abilities of its king!

? *Read Dt. 17:19–20. Explain the purpose of requiring the king to study Torah for life. Describe the relationship between studying Torah and the promise of an everlasting dynasty for the line of the king.*

The Priestly Inheritance

> ❝ *The cohanim, . . . and indeed the whole tribe of Levi, is not to have a share or an inheritance with Isra'el. Instead, their support will come from the food offered by fire to ADONAI . . .* ❞ —Dt. 18:1

As the next generation matures into the responsibilities of the priesthood, Torah elevates all L'vi'im (*Levites*), not just the sons of Aharon, to priestly ministry (cf. Lev. 6 ff.).

All L'vi'im live off the tithes of the nation.

All L'vi'im receive portions of sacrificial animals and firstfruits. But they receive no land inheritance; the LORD is their portion (Dt. 18:1–2). The same tasks previously divided between L'vi'im and kohanim (Num. 18:1–7) now appear to be assigned, without distinction, to any Levite serving as priest in the sanctuary [Dt. 18:3–5; Tigay, p. 170].

Once in the Land, not every lay person can reach the sanctuary to offer a zevach sh'lamim (*sacrifice of well-being*). It is no longer possible to tithe all breasts and right thighs to kohanim at that central location (Lev. 7:28–34). When animals are slaughtered by laity for food, the L'vi'im receive their assigned dues [Dt. 18:3; Tigay, p. 171; M. Chul. 10:1].

? Read Dt. 18:1–2, cf. Lev. 7:28–36; Num. 18:9, 20. Discuss whether the absence of a distinction between Levites and priests is a new change for the new generation or merely superfluous since Sefer D'VARIM addresses the laity, not clergy.

The Kohanim

> **"** *If a Levi from one of your towns anywhere in Isra'el where he is living comes, highly motivated, to the place which* ADONAI *will choose, then he will serve there in the name of* ADONAI *...* **"**—Dt. 18:6–7a

L'vi'im may journey from their settlements to the central sanctuary to minister b'shem ADONAI (*in the name of the* LORD, Dt. 18:7). The sages agree that the Levite choir imparted a unique ministry in the Temple, singing to the LORD.

However, majority opinion argues that only the kohanim ate the sacrifices chelek k'chelek (*portion by portion*, Dt. 18:8f) in the Temple [Rashi, Sifre, Rambam, Arach. 11a]. Chazal references 24 places in Torah where kohanim are called L'vi'im [Yev. 86b]. It is argued that the seg-ment begins by talking about the entire tribe of Levi, but then narrows down to the kohanim, who may wish to offer personal sacrifices when they journey to Y'rushalayim.

Go to God's place— trust, rejoice and worship!

But all Yisra'el must avoid soothsaying to determine future events, such as divining when the rains will come in order to sow at the proper time (Dt. 18:9–13). Yisra'el must practice a faith that trusts God wholeheartedly!

? *Read Dt. 18:13. Note the words tamim tih'yeh (whole-hearted shall you be). God told Avram, "Walk . . . and be pure-hearted!" (Gen. 17:1). Relate wholeheartedness to covenant faith and trusting God for rain.*

The Prophet!

> **" For these nations, which you are about to dispossess, listen to soothsayers and diviners; but you, ADONAI your God does not allow you to do this. "**
> —Deuteronomy 18:14

Gentiles divine the future from consulting soothsayers and astrologers; but God provides Yisra'el a navi (*prophet*) like Himself . . . elav tishma'un (*to him shall you listen*, Dt. 18:15).

Listen only to My Voice, spoken by My prophet!

At Sinai, Yisra'el stood at a distance, trembled, and told Moshe, "You, speak with us; and we will listen. But don't let God speak with us, or we will die" (Ex. 20:19(16רמ״ד)). God raises the navi as proclaimer of His Voice (Dt. 18:18).

The people must hear and obey the navi, and they must put to death any prophet who speaks with presumption (Dt. 18:20, 22). Thus, the Sinai experience is institutionalized as an ever-present reality. God raises up prophets to speak His Voice and guide Yisra'el. No other way to divine the future is permitted!

The rest of this segment addresses cities of refuge and matters of capital punishment. No mercy can be shown by the go'el (*redeemer*) to the one who hates and then sheds innocent blood (Dt. 19:13).

? *Starting at Sinai, God speaks so the people will believe in Him and in His prophet Moshe. Read Dt. 18:15, 18–19; cf. Mt. 17:5, Jn. 5:45–47, 12:48–50, Ac. 3:22–24, 7:37. Explain how the B'rit Chadashah builds on Moshe's office.*

Boundary Lines

❝ *You are not to move your neighbor's boundary marker from the place where people put it long ago, in the inheritance soon to be yours in the land . . . God is giving you to possess.* ❞ 　　　　—Dt. 19:14

Inheritances received from the LORD, such as tribal holdings and borders, are deemed sacred. Moving boundary markers is explicitly cursed by God as a violation of the covenant (Dt. 27:17). It is noteworthy that the topic of apportioning cities of refuge (Dt. 19:1–13) is juxtaposed with the topic of encroachment on property (Dt. 19:14).

Inheritances are sacred trusts reserved for future generations.

This segment addresses the issue of witnesses to crimes. On the testimony of two or three witnesses, a davar (*legal matter*) can be established (Dt. 19:15, cf. Mt. 18:19–20). The principle of midot k'neged midot (*measure for measure*) applies to the testimony of false witnesses: the one who falsely plots will reap ka'asher zamam la'asot l'achiv (*just as he schemed to do to his brother*, Dt. 19:19).

Once more, the text demands the relentless pursuit of justice. Burn evil out of Israel! Deter! Show no pity for these kinds of offenses (Dt. 19:19–21).

The rest of the segment describes army preparations for war against enemies (Dt. 20:1–9).

Read Dt. 19:15. Consider the start of the Kol Nidrei service of Yom Kippur, when two people hold Torahs, and a third person, the cantor, annuls all vows. How does this affect your understanding of believers' courts in Mt. 18:15–20?

Rules of War

> ❝ *When you advance on a town to attack it, first offer it terms for peace. If it accepts the terms . . . then all the people there are to be put to forced labor and work for you* ❞ —Deuteronomy 20:10–11

Peace offers precede the waging of war! Should the town surrender and open its gates, Torah instructs Yisra'el to take forced laborers (Dt. 20:11). But should the town determine to fight, Yisra'el is to put all males to the sword, then absorb the women, infants, animals, and booty into its households.

In the case of the seven Canaanite tribes in the Land, however, these tribes are accursed of God and subject to the ban: the Hittite, Amorite, Canaanite, Perizzite, Hivvite, and Yevusite must be destroyed—wiped out completely (Dt. 20:17, cf. Gen. 9:24–25). Except for the fruit trees, everything must go (Dt. 20:14, 19).

Jihad applies to Canaanite idolaters who sacrifice their sons to the fire God.

Relativists will never understand how idolatry and the abominations that accompany it can be viewed by a loving God as an absolute evil (Dt. 20:17–18). Yet Canaanite idolatry hardened into child sacrifice, a kind of ritual murder God prohibited.

? *Review Gen. 22:10–13, 16–18. Explain how God challenged Avraham to contemplate the ritual murder of Yitzchak, his heir . . . only to stop him and reveal that his inheritance is guaranteed by the sworn oath of God Himself.*

Redeeming Bloodshed

> ❝ Thus you will banish the shedding of innocent blood from among you, by doing what ADONAI sees as right. ❞
>
> —Deuteronomy 21:9

The nation is called to cleanse the Land by banishing bloodshed. Kayin was the first accursed for shedding the innocent blood of his brother (Gen. 4:11). Blood defiles the Land, because the life in the blood cries out to God for justice!

Cleansing the Land fills it with the glory of God.

In the case of an unconfessed murder, the nearest town's elders must execute justice or declare their innocence by washing their hands at the site (Dt. 21:6–7). God calls Yisra'el to set up a just society "atoned of the blood" and pursue justice, so that "you yourself burn out the innocent blood from your midst" (Fox, Dt. 21:8–9). In this way, ta'aseh ha-yashar (*you will do the right thing*) in God's sight (Dt. 21:9). From "yashar," Yisra'el's nickname Y'shurun (*Little Straight One*) can be derived (cf. Dt. 32:15, 33:5, 26, Is. 44:2).

Failure to purge the Land of murderers ultimately defiles the Land and drives God from the camp. Without protection, enemies prey upon Yisra'el, and the curses of the covenant fall upon her.

？ Notice that "burning out the innocent blood" is stressed in this parashah (Dt. 19:13; 21:9). Note Mt. 23:35–36.
• Discuss how Yisra'el's spiritual failure to atone for the sin of Kayin defiles the Land and curses the nation, too.

Judge, King, and Redeemer

Meander

> **❝ I, yes I, am the one who comforts you! Why are you afraid of a man, who must die; of a human being, who will wither like grass? ❞**
>
> —Isaiah 51:12

Ever so tenderly, God Himself speaks to Yisra'el: Anochi, Anochi hu m'nachemchem (*I, I am He who comforts you*, Is. 51:12).

God personally comes to comfort His people.

ADONAI personally comes to His storm-tossed and unconsoled city (cf. Is. 54:11, 49:14, 40:1). Though His bride, Y'rushalayim, had forgotten the one who made her, God comes anyhow (Is. 51:13, cf. Dt. 32:6d, 19). He awakens His bride from the stupor resulting when Y'rushalayim drank deeply from His cup of wrath (Is. 51:17, 21; cf. Dt. 32:36–38). Now, the enemies of Y'rushalayim stagger from drinking the very same cup!

The enemies had afflicted Y'rushalayim with a judgment far beyond what God had intended. Now the enemies reap what deeds they have sown (Is. 51:23; cf. Dt. 32:40–43).

As for Y'rushalayim, God returns His Presence to the city. He escorts the exiles, going before them and behind them in a slow, but holy, processional which contrasts with the hasty exodus from Egypt (Is. 52:12).

? Read Is. 51:17, 19, 21; cf. Dt. 32:36–38. Explain the trouble coming upon Y'rushalayim for drinking the cup of God's wrath. Relate the role of suffering to atonement and redemption. Read Is. 52:3. How does God redeem His people?

> **"** *. . . heaven was opened, he saw the Spirit of God coming down upon him like a dove, and a voice from heaven said, "This is my Son, whom I love; I am well pleased with him."* **"**   —Matthew 3:16–17

Yochanan, clothed in the garments of Eliyahu, proclaims repentance to prepare the way of the LORD (Mt. 3:4, 6; cf. 2 Ki. 1:8). Proclamation begins at Beit-Anyah (*Bethany, house of poverty*), a village outside the Land, east of the Yarden (Jn. 1:28).

Repent and return to the city of God.

Yochanan calls the people to repentance and holy living. God is Present, going before and behind His people, as the grand, holy processional moves from exile to Y'rushalayim (cf. Is. 52:9–12). Indeed, God sends His Son as the suffering servant (Is. 42:1).

People come from all directions, including Y'rushalayim (Mt. 3:5, 13). Thus, it comes as no surprise when Yeshua asks Yochanan to immerse him at the Yarden, entry point into the Land. To fulfill all righteousness, Yochanan agrees. Suddenly, the heavens open. The Ruach descends. A Voice from heaven announces the coming of God's very own Son (Mt. 3:17; cf. Is. 42:1, Mt. 17:5).

? Re-read Is. 42:1, cf. Mt. 3:17. Would Yeshua have understood these words to be his mission as suffering servant?
• Note that Yeshua's ministry started across the Yarden. What part of Is. 52:9–12 is not yet fulfilled?

Talk Your Walk . . .

G reat institutions for a just society include provisions for judges and officials to enforce their decrees, priests to instruct the people, and prophets to speak the word of God into situations when men fail their assignments. Only the office of king is optional. Here, God reserves the right to appoint the king through His prophet. Land inheritances with secure borders are sacred trusts conveyed across generations. The Land must remain free of bloodshed, lest God follow His people into exile.

The Haftarah picks up with God and His people in exile, as a result of idolatry, immorality, and bloodshed. Yisra'el is punished doubly by her enemies. God comes personally to comfort His people in exile and lead them back in holy procession to Y'rushalayim. He raises up Medo-Persian rulers, first Cyrus and then Darius, to direct the return. In contrast to the Exodus from Egypt, this procession is slow, but holy. Temple implements return with the priests, with blessing from on high and from the secular empire.

> **God sends Messiah to personally comfort His people, Yisra'el.**

The B'rit Chadashah continues the thrust of the Haftarah. God sends Messiah to Beit-Anyah. He enters the waters of purification from exile, leading by example. Purity is prominent. God signals that the Prophet like Moshe comes to lead the people: "This is my Son . . . I am well pleased with him" (Mt. 3:17; Dt. 18:15).

Oasis

. . . Walk Your Talk

Have you ever desired God alone to comfort you? The quality of your quiet time is tested during moments such as these. Are you willing to abide in peace with Him, surrendering your pains and losses to be forever forgotten by all except Him? It may cost you those things that you value most! But then, shouldn't you really value Him most?

Remember, He is the guarantor of justice, not the human institutions and people surrounding you. Mankind will fail you. Only God knows the real truth, and only God cares enough to preserve those things which you value most.

But the universe is a complicated place. Rest assured that God measures out to others what they measure out to you. Their time will come. If you think that the standards expected of you are higher than the standards expected of others, do not be fooled and do not despair.

> *God wills to sanctify life, filling heaven and earth with everlasting glory.*

God was pleased to crush Messiah, so that His purposes might be made complete in you. Can you let Him try your soul, in order to make you pure?

 **Shabbat Shalom!**

When you go out to war,
כִּי תֵצֵא,
haShem will lead you
to fight His way.
Wage holy war,
do not stray.
Take towns and captives
everyday.

All newlyweds
can take a bye,
to honeymoon
and multiply.
But if 'Amalek
should be the guy—
they must blot HIM out
without a sigh!

Walk KI TETSE!
21:10–25:19

כִּי תֵצֵא

When you go out

TORAH—Deuteronomy 21:10–25:19

HAFTARAH—Isaiah 54:1–10

Barren Y'rushalayim—Isaiah 54:1

B'RIT CHADASHAH—1 Corinthians 5:1–5

Atonement through Death!—1 Corinthians 5:5

Going Out to War

Hiker's

⬅ Looking Back

B'REISHEET (*in the beginning*), God creates paradise. But man disobeys, and God scatters him into the seventy nations of the world. Seventy **SH'MOT** (*names*) list Ya'akov's sons, whom God reunites in Egypt and multiplies to nationhood. After 400 years of slavery, He redeems us to serve as a holy nation.

VAYIKRA (*and called*) the LORD to Moshe from the Tent of Meeting to come learn how Yisra'el is to walk in purity and minister in His dwelling. **B'MIDBAR** (*in the wilderness of*) Sinai, Yisra'el follows God's cloud, marching as a nation guided by ADONAI. But the fathers fail to confront the giants, and disobedience incurs divine wrath.

Moshe's **D'VARIM** (*words*) exhort the new generation to enter the Land and appropriate their God-given inheri-

> In final **D'VARIM**, *Moshe says:*
> "**VA'ET'CHANAN**, *but you must enter the Land without me.*
> **EKEV** *your obedience,*
> *God will make you fruitful!*
> **R'EH**, *choose the path of blessing so you don't wind up D-E-A-D."*
>
> "*Appoint* **SHOF'TIM**—*judges for a just society.*
> **KI TETSE**—*when you go out to war, stay connected to God."*

tance. Moshe urges Yisra'el to obey so she will enjoy long life in the Land. He recounts the sins of the fathers and exhorts the children, now grown, to face the giants and not shrink from the calling their fathers feared.

Moshe describes how he entreated God: **VA'ET'CHANAN** (*and I pleaded*) with tears to enter the Land, but God refused. Moshe exhorts the sons of Yisra'el to obey Torah,

Log

lest they die in exile, too. He warns that chosenness does not mean favoritism.

Rather, **EKEV** (*as a result of*) their exacting obedience, God will transform the universe and even send hornets to chase Yisra'el's enemies. Prosperity depends on obedience. **R'EH** (*see!*) two paths lie ahead: one leads to blessings and long life in the Land; whereas the other leads to a DEAD end—destruction, exile, assimilation, and death— with loss of sovereignty, followed by indentured service to foreign idols!

To avoid the pitfalls, we must appoint **SHOF'TIM** (*judges*) and create a just society. Judges must pursue justice with passion. Priests instruct the nation to listen to God's Voice. Prophets serve to check and balance the king, priests, elders, courts, and

In KI TETSE . . .

The Key Person is Moshe (*Moses*), speaking to all Yisra'el (*Israel*).

The Scene is the wilderness east of the Promised Land, ready to cross over the Yarden (*Jordan*).

Main Events include more of Moshe's words about: marrying women prisoners of war, rights of a firstborn, consequences for a rebellious son, miscellaneous laws, tsitsit, sexual purity, restrictions on joining the assembly, avoiding impurities, more laws about loans, vows, divorce, newlyweds, skin diseases, poor people, business practices, and removal of Amalekites.

society. Most importantly, the ground must be kept clean, undefiled from bloodshed.

Moshe next turns his attention to how we should act during war. **KI TETSE** (*when you go out*) . . .

The Trail Ahead

The Path

כִּי תֵצֵא לַמִּלְחָמָה עַל אֹיְבֶיךָ
וּנְתָנוֹ יְהוָה אֱלֹהֶיךָ בְּיָדֶךָ
וְשָׁבִיתָ שִׁבְיוֹ

—דברים כא/י

א	צֵ	תֵ	־	י	כִּ
letter: alef	tsadee	tav		yod	kaf
sound: (silent)	**TSei**	Tei		EE	Kee

when you go out = KI TETSE = **כִּי תֵצֵא**

Work

The Legend

<u>When you go out</u>	*ki tetse*	כִּי־תֵצֵא
to war	*la-milchamah*	לַמִּלְחָמָה
against enemies-your,	*al-o-y'vecha*	עַל־אֹיְבֶיךָ
and gives him	*oo-n'tanoh*	וּנְתָנוֹ
the LORD God-your	*ADONAI Eloheicha*	יְהֹוָה אֱלֹהֶיךָ
into hand-your	*b'yadecha*	בְּיָדֶךָ
and you capture	*v'shavita*	וְשָׁבִיתָ
captives-his . . .	*shiv'yoh*	שִׁבְיוֹ׃

—*Deuteronomy 21:10*

Related Words

and he went out (Gen. 28:10)	*va-yetse*	וַיֵּצֵא
to go out, leave, expire, be exempt, defecate	*yatsa*	יָצָא
exit, departure, emigration, death, expense	*y'tsiah*	יְצִיאָה
the Exodus from Egypt	*y'tsiat Mitsrayim*	יְצִיאַת מִצְרַיִם
extraordinary (went out from the rule)	*yatsa min ha-c'lal*	יָצָא מִן הַכְּלָל
blessing for bread coming forth from the earth	*ha-motsi*	הַמּוֹצִיא
for from Zion goes out (the) Torah	*ki mi-Tsiyon tetse Torah*	כִּי מִצִּיּוֹן תֵּצֵא תוֹרָה

Hit the Trail!

Going Out to Capture

❝ When you go out to war against your enemies, and ADONAI your God hands them over to you, and you take prisoners, . . . ❞

—*Deuteronomy 21:10*

The parashah KI TETSE begins and ends with the imagery of *going out* to war (Dt. 21:10, 25:17–19). In between, seventy-four mitsvot address miscellaneous laws of the covenant.

Three laws govern family matters.

These stipulations address private matters in civil and domestic life, in contrast to the previous parashah which dealt with public matters affecting the nation. This parashah is packed with more than six times the number of mitsvot in an average portion.

The present segment details laws governing a husband's treatment of a captive wife (Dt. 21:10–14), the rights of the firstborn from an unloved wife (Dt. 21:15–17), and the adolescent son who is intolerably insubordinate (Dt. 21:18–21). Should the parents warn the rebel son, report him as a glutton and a drunkard, and say, "einenu shomea b'kolenu (*he does not listen to our voice*)," then Torah orders the townsmen to stone the son to death. Thus, biarta ha-ra' mi-kirbecha (*you will burn out the evil from your midst*, Dt. 21:21).

?• *Talmud describes the meal of the rebellious son. He steals money, drinks wine, and exits the family's property to eat raw meat with blood (cf. Pr. 28:7, 23:20–21). No son was ever stoned [Sanh. 71a]. Explain why Torah includes this law.*

Sins that Kill

> ❝ If someone has committed a capital crime and is put to death, then hung on a tree, his body is not to remain all night on the tree, but you must bury him the same day . . . ❞ —Deuteronomy 21:22–23a

Capital offenses require execution and burial by sunset (Dt. 21:22–23, cf. Mt. 27:57–61). A hanging man is a curse to God. According to Talmud, an executed criminal would be hung by the hands just before sunset and then taken down again for burial [Yad, Sanh. 15:7]. Failure to bury before sunset defiles the ground; thus, Y'hoshua took care to bury the bodies of Canaanite kings (Dt. 21:23, cf. Josh. 8:29, 10:27).

Miscellaneous domestic laws now follow, mostly related to property. Torah requires acts of kindness and decency concerning lost and fallen animals (Dt. 22:1–4), clothing of the opposite sex (Dt. 22:5), and finally a fallen bird's nest (Dt. 22:6–7).

Acts of kindness engender compassion and dignity.

To exterminate the mother along with the young, though common in war situations, was also cruel. Torah requires that the mother be chased away, rather than eaten with the young. Thus, Hebrew sensitivities of showing kindness across generations also extend to animals.

? Read Dt. 21:22–23; cf. Mt. 27:22–25, 57–61. Does "hanging" put the curses of the covenant on Yeshua? Explain Yeshua's role as sin-bearer. Is putting his blood on our heads and the heads of our children a "sin of the fathers"?

Unwholesome Behaviors

> ❝ When you build a new house, you must build a low wall around your roof; otherwise someone may fall from it, and you will be responsible for his death. ❞
> —Deuteronomy 22:8

Unwholesome roofs can cause people to fall (Dt. 22:8). Torah also prohibits unwholesome mixtures in domestic matters such as seeding, plowing, and clothing (Dt. 22:9–11).

Unwholesome mixes lack integrity.

Unwholesome conduct in marriage includes dishonesty and sexual misconduct in matters of adultery, seduction, and rape (Dt. 22:13–29). Unwholesome households include those with people in forbidden relationships or suffering from impaired fertility or giving birth to a mamzer (*product of a forbidden marriage*, Dt. 22:30– 23:2(23:1–3‏תנ״ך‎)).

Finally, Torah addresses the effects of the sins of the fathers on future generations. Consequences for inhospitable behaviors are severe (Num. 22:2–6; cf. Gen. 18–19). As a result of hostility to Yisra'el en route to the Land, heads of Ammonite and Moabite households are banned from citizenship and intermarriage for ten generations [Dt. 23:3–6 (4–7‏תנ״ך‎); Tigay, p. 211].

> **?** Contrast Avraham's hospitality and his destiny with Lot's hospitality and the loss of half his household (Gen. 18–19). Explain how sins of Moabite and Ammonite fathers affect the sons for ten generations (Dt. 23:3–6(4–7‏תנ״ך‎)).

Sins of the Fathers

> **❝ But you are not to detest an Edomi, because he is your brother; and you are not to detest an Egyptian, because you lived as a foreigner in his land. ❞**
> —Deuteronomy 23:7(8‏תנ״ך‏)

In contrast to Ammonites and Moabites, Edomites and Egyptians are banned only to the third generation. Thus, their grandchildren can enter the assembly of ADONAI (Dt. 23:8(9‏תנ״ך‏)).

Considering that Mo'av, Ammon, Edom, and Egypt collectively fail to feed or protect Yisra'el when she passes through "their" God-given land inheritances, perhaps a certain logic of case law can be seen. Torah refers to Yisra'el as Edom's brother (Num 20:14; Dt. 2:4, cf. Obad. 10, Mal. 1:2), despite the treacherous past (Gen. 25–27, 32–33). Initially, Egypt showed hospitality, despite a bitter end (Gen 47).

> *Some sins can be forgiven more easily than others.*

Topics closing this segment include standards in a military camp, asylum for escaped slaves, rules for lending, and keeping one's word. Miscellaneous laws continue to span the next four chapters (Dt. 23–26). They expand on the themes of marriage, giving crops to strangers, protecting the disadvantaged, etc.

> **?** *Read Gen. 45:16–20, 50:4–9, Ex. 1:1–11. Note how the Egyptians treated Yisra'el when she was a vulnerable household of seventy persons (Ex. 1:5). Despite the later problems, explain God's kindness to the fathers of Egypt.*

Laborers

> **❝** When you enter your neighbor's vineyard, you may eat enough grapes to satisfy your appetite; but you are not to put any in your basket. **❞**
> —Deuteronomy 23:24(25‑תנ״ך)

Workers receive the rights to slake momentary thirst and hunger. You may eat k'naf'sh'cha sav'echa ("to satisfy your appetite," Dt. 23:24 (25‑תנ״ך)), but not to satiate by filling yourself up completely!

> ### *Practice moderation and compassion for laborers.*

Thus, Torah strikes a balance between needs and theft. Laborers in the fields may not stuff themselves or their baskets, nor can they harvest standing grain for personal use (Dt. 23:25–26(26–27‑תנ״ך)).

The last of the segment moves on to limit the right of remarriage for those who divorce (Dt. 24:1–4). Torah stipulates that the first bill of divorce be based on ervat davar (*something of 'nakedness,'* Fox transl. of Dt. 24:1; cf. Dt. 23:15). If the woman marries another and this marriage also ends in formal divorce, then the first husband cannot take back his former wife (Dt. 24:3–4). In fact, remarriage is called an abomination that defiles the Land: v'lo tachati et-ha-aretz (*do not bring sin upon the Land,* Dt. 24:4).

? Read Dt. 24:4 and review Is. 50:1. How important is it that God did not formally divorce His people when He exiled them for idolatry? Explain how Yisra'el's cure from idolatry in Babylon enables God to renew His covenant.

Newlyweds

> " *If a man has recently married his wife, he is not to be subject to military service; he is to be free of external obligations and left at home for one year to make his new wife happy.* " —Deuteronomy 24:5

One-year exemptions from military service apply to newlyweds, to those who have moved to a new home, and to those who have redeemed a new vineyard. In the case of the newlywed, Torah obligates the husband with the words simach et-ishto (*he shall gladden his wife*, Dt. 24:5).

Blessing accrues to those who avoid taking unfair advantage.

Stone [p. 1059] comments, "...a man does not experience true joy unless he brings joy to others." Torah places a value on sexuality in newlywed life, not just bearing children. Interestingly, the millstone in Dt. 24:6 can also be used as a metaphor for sexual relations on account of its grinding property (cf. Job. 31:10).

Five items mentioned in this segment can be withheld: the new husband withheld from the army (Dt. 24:5); and a millstone, a disadvantaged person, a house, or a vitally needed garment, all withheld from a creditor trying to extort loan paybacks (Dt. 24:6–13). Torah says that those who respect these laws will receive ts'dakah (*righteous merit*) with God (Dt. 24:13).

? Read Dt. 24:8–9; cf. Num. 12:1–15. How does God respond to gossip and slander? Review the parable of the marriage supper (Lk. 14:15–24, esp. vv. 18–20). Discuss the impact of taking or not taking unfair advantage of others.

Hired Hands

❝ You are not to exploit a hired worker who is poor and needy, whether one of your brothers or a foreigner living in your land in your town. ❞

—*Deuteronomy 24:14*

Here, Torah advises employers to avoid extorting unfair advantages for personal gains. Thus, an employer is not to exploit a hired worker or an indentured servant by withholding wages (Dt. 24:14–15, cf. Lev. 19:13). Sunset marks the deadline for wages paid, lest God curse the unfair employer when the needy cry out to Him (Dt. 24:15).

Eighteen mitzvot are covered in this segment, with frequent appeals not to degrade a brother or pervert justice or take unfair advantage of society's weaker members.

Jews, once downtrodden in Egypt but then redeemed by God, must always remember their former state and not pass on elements of slavery or despotic rule (Dt. 24:18).

> *Curses follow those who extort unjust gains from the vulnerable.*

Thus, the one who cheats the widow, orphan, or alien; the one who harvests every bundle; the one who favors the wicked, strikes the weak, seizes another's inheritance, or uses dishonest weights— all these incur the curse of the law for unjust gains.

Review the basis for Israelite generosity to the widow, orphan, alien, and poor (Ex. 22:21–27(20–26תה"ו), Dt. 24:19–22). Explain how Yisra'el's oppression of the downtrodden brought the curse of the law upon the nation (cf. Amos 2:6–8).

'Amalek

> **"** . . . *when* ADONAI . . . *has given you rest from all your surrounding enemies in the land . . . God is giving you . . . you are to blot out all memory of 'Amalek from under heaven. Don't forget!* **"**   —Dt. 25:19

As God blotted out the line of Kayin during the Great Flood, now Yisra'el must blot out the copycat evil twin nation!

> ### God co-partners with Yisra'el to blot out evil.

Recall that Timna, granddaughter to Se'ir, a Horite, wished to mother a great nation that would live forever. To marry into Avraham's line, she became a concubine to Elifaz, son of Esav. This union produced a son, 'Amalek, crossing a Canaanite with the line of Esav, Ya'akov's twin who despised his birthright (Gen. 25:34; 36:12, 40–43).

'Amalek matures into a tribe that has no fear of the LORD (Dt. 25:18), which becomes self evident after the Exodus. When Yisra'el left Egypt triumphantly, most nations quaked in fear over the manifest power of God! But 'Amalek punctured some of this awe by preying upon elderly and children at the rearguard of the company near R'fidim (Ex. 17:8, 13–16).

Thus, the LORD decreed, ". . . blot out all memory of 'Amalek from under heaven. Don't forget!" (Dt. 25:19).

> **?** *Read 1 Samuel 15, cf. Dt. 25:19. Comment on how Sha'ul failed to heed the words of Torah, spoken by God.*
> • *Explain how, measure for measure, King Sha'ul lost his dynasty because he spared 'Amalek's king in battle.*

Barren
Y'rushalayim
Meander

> ❝ *Sing, barren woman who has never had a child!*
> *Burst into song, shout for joy . . . For the deserted*
> *wife will have more children than the woman who*
> *is living with her husband . . .* ❞ — **Isaiah 54:1**

Y'rushalayim, with her children in exile, is compared to a woman who never bore a child (Is. 54:1, cf. Is. 49:21). God tells her to enlarge her tent and prepare many places for many children (Is. 54:2).

Homecoming! "'I was angry for a moment and hid my face from you; but with everlasting grace I will have compassion on you,' says ADONAI your Redeemer" (Is. 54:8). Tenderly, the Redeemer brings back the children to barren Y'rushalayim. Promises are fulfilled, and the days of Messiah commence!

A new promise accompanies the presence of Messiah. As God once promised never again to destroy the world as He did in the days of Noach, He now takes the oath, ". . . so now I swear that never again will I be angry with you or rebuke you" (Is. 54:9).

God promises never again to hide His face.

Y'rushalayim emerges from the furnace of affliction, and her sufferings are made the crucible for a future glory that celebrates fruitful blessings (Is. 54:10).

? Read Is. 54:6–8, cf. Dt. 32:20, Mt. 24:37, 43. Why does God hide His face? What consequences follow? Read Is. 54:10.
● Explain God's oath in the Days of Messiah, that He will never again be angry with nor rebuke His people, Yisra'el.

> " ... *hand over such a person to the Adversary for his old nature to be destroyed, so that his spirit may be saved in the Day of the Lord.* "
>
> — *1 Corinthians 5:5*

Aristophanes (450–385 BCE) first coined the term Korinaiazo (*to act like a Corinthian, to commit fornication*) to describe the lawless behavior of citizens from the wealthy port town of Corinth. Rav Sha'ul advises corporate surgery and, if necessary, excommunication for believers under church discipline (1 Cor. 5:11). Those judged for immorality (e.g., incest, 1 Cor. 5:1, Dt. 23:1(22:30חצר)) must be removed from the assemblies for worship, fellowship meals, and S'udat haAdon (*the Lord's Supper*). Thus, Rav Sha'ul urges the believers to put those under discipline into Satan's domain for the destruction of the flesh (1 Jn. 5:16–19, 1 Cor. 11:30).

Suffering unto death can bring redemption.

Ironically, the purpose of exclusion is redemptive. Expulsion does not lead to damnation, but rather to admonishment (2 Thes. 3:14). Nor can condoning sin lead to final salvation. Thus, the purpose of expulsion as discipline is not to punish, but rather to reform [Robertson, p. 113].

? • *Read 2 Cor. 12:7–10. Explain how Rav Sha'ul calls his suffering a "messenger of Satan." Read 1 Cor. 11:27–32, 1 Jn. 5:16–17, cf. 1 Cor. 5:5. How can unworthily eating the Lord's Supper be a sin that leads "not to death"?*

Talk Your Walk . . .

The covenant requires Yisra'el to extend love and offer compassion when going out, whether to war or to address private matters of civil and domestic life. But for the immoral nation that chooses to harden itself, the parashah closes with a divine order to blot out 'Amalek, the evil twin nation that champions Edomite and Canaanite hatred of God. In living co-partnership with God, Yisra'el must cleanse the Land of all defilement from idolatry and immorality in order to enter her inheritance.

> **Both suffering and repentance bring change.**

The Haftarah continues the theme that God comes personally to redeem Y'rushalayim, his abandoned bride, barren of children, and suffering in exile. He calls upon Y'rushalayim to expand her tent and prepare for the return of many, many children. God swears an oath to never again be angry at or rebuke His people.

The B'rit Chadashah expands on the salutary effects of disciplining the immoral. Believers judged for immorality must be removed from assemblies with the hope that those who suffer in exile will seek salvation in the Day of the LORD. Whether immorality arises from war, adultery, or idolatry, suffering major loss can cleanse, bringing atonement to those who are purified by their suffering. When repentance is incomplete, an all-knowing, all-powerful God can use godly discipline to bring about godly outcomes.

Conclusion

Oasis

. . . Walk Your Talk

Many of us have relatives who harden themselves against repentance, choosing instead to war against God. How can one abide in "the peace that passes all understanding," yet not give up on witnessing Messiah's love to beloved family members? Over time, attempts to witness can be misperceived as our personal agenda, rather than a showing of our love and compassion. Is this fair?

Our relatives' misconceptions also paint us into a corner. We feel guilty about consigning loved ones to a fate that excludes the love of God. Alternatively, any failure to nurse the guilt leaves us with thoughts that we are heartlessly lacking in compassion and giving up on family members who are hopelessly lost.

Where is God's peace in our lives when we face the Scylla of guilt and the Charybdis of heartlessness? Must we suffer so, because our families choose to harden against God?

A third alternative remains. We can be present for loved ones in times of crisis. We can

Suffering can change lives.

pray, and we can be spiritually strong. Consider how you can wait in peace until God opens doors.

Shabbat Shalom!

When you enter in,
כִּי תָבוֹא,
tithe the first
of the fruits you sow.
Tell the priest my dad
was on the go,
a wanderin' Aramean
down and out, really low.

But now God is blessing
the accursed ground.
Where thorns are dying,
now fruits abound!
So enter the Land
where blessings are found.
Rejoice in God—
make a mighty sound!

Walk KI TAVO!
26:1–29:9(8תנ״ך)

כִּי תָבוֹא
When you enter in

TORAH—Deuteronomy 26:1–29:9(8תנ״ך)
- 1st Entering into Prosperity—Deuteronomy 26:1–2a
- 2nd Eat Nothing Holy!—Deuteronomy 26:12–13a
- 3rd Ascending on High—Deuteronomy 26:16
- 4th Nationhood—Deuteronomy 27:1
- 5th Covenant Renewal—Deuteronomy 27:11–13
- 6th Invincibility—Deuteronomy 28:7
- 7th Eyes to See—Deuteronomy 29:2(1תנ״ך)
- Maftir Inheriting—Deuteronomy 29:9(8תנ״ך)

HAFTARAH—Isaiah 60:1–22
- Days of Glory—Isaiah 60:1–2

B'RIT CHADASHAH—Luke 24:44–53
- Firstfruits Redeemed—Luke 24:51–53

Entering Into the Covenant

← Looking Back

B'REISHEET (*in the beginning*), God's paradise crashes when man disobeys. God scatters him into seventy nations. Seventy sons, whose SH'MOT (*names*) are listed, God reunites, multiplies, redeems, and calls to serve in His house as a kingdom of priests and a holy nation.

vaYIKRA ADONAI (*and the LORD called*) to Moshe. He gives instructions for his firstborn son, Yisra'el, to walk in purity and minister in His dwelling. B'MIDBAR (*in the wilderness of*) Sinai, Yisra'el surrounds God's dwelling. But the fathers' failure to confront the giants incurs wrath from God.

Moshe's final D'VARIM (*words*) exhort the new generation to enter the Promised Land! Three sermons urge Yisra'el to obey, so she may enjoy long life in the Land.

Moshe recounts the sins of the fathers, urging the new generation to face the giants and appropriate the nation's inheritance.

In final D'VARIM, *Moshe says:*
"VA'ET'CHANAN, *but you must enter the Land without me.*
EKEV *your obedience,*
God will make you fruitful!
R'EH, *choose the path of blessing so you don't wind up D-E-A-D.*
Appoint SHOF'TIM—*judges for a just society."*

"KI TETSE—*when you go out to war, stay connected to God.*
Then KI TAVO—*when you enter in, offer firstfruits to God!"*

Moshe reminds his people: VA'ET'CHANAN (*and I pleaded*) to enter, but God refused. Moshe exhorts Yisra'el to obey Torah, lest they die in exile. He warns them that chosenness does not mean favoritism. Rather, it is EKEV

Log

(*as a result of*) exacting obedience that God will transform the universe and send hornets to chase away Yisra'el's enemies. Prosperity also depends on obedience to God's commands.

R'EH (*see!*), two paths lie ahead. One path leads to blessings and long life in the Land; whereas the other path leads to a DEAD end—<u>d</u>estruction, <u>e</u>xile, <u>a</u>ssimilation, and <u>d</u>eath as a nation.

Moshe urges us to appoint SHOF'TIM (*judges*). Pursuit of justice with passion ensures a just society. Priests instruct the nation and live off tithes. Prophets hear God's Voice and balance out the institutions of society.

Moshe goes on to say that KI TETSE (*when you go out*) to war, you should offer peace first. Maintain integrity in all

> **In KI TAVO . . .**
> **The Key Person** is Moshe (*Moses*), speaking to all Yisra'el (*Israel*).
> **The Scene** is the wilderness east of the Promised Land, ready to cross over the Yarden (*Jordan*).
> **Main Events** include Moshe's words about what to do when you enter into the Land: offer firstfruits and tithes, obey God's commands, inscribe Torah on stones, and proclaim blessings for obeying from Mt. G'rizim (*Gerizim*) and curses for disobeying from Mt. Eival (*Ebal*); covenant renewal and invincibility as God keeps His chesed (*covenant kindness*).

relationships, especially with society's vulnerable, the laborers, newlyweds, and hired hands. But to 'Amalek, show no compassion. Blot out evil!

Then, KI TAVO (*when you enter in*) to the Land of Promise and appropriate God's inheritance . . .

The Trail Ahead

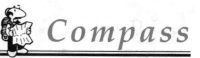

Compass

The Path

וְהָיָה כִּי תָבוֹא אֶל הָאָרֶץ
אֲשֶׁר יְהֹוָה אֱלֹהֶיךָ
נֹתֵן לְךָ נַחֲלָה
וִירִשְׁתָּהּ וְיָשַׁבְתָּ בָּהּ
וְלָקַחְתָּ מֵרֵאשִׁית כָּל פְּרִי

—דברים כו/א-ב

	א	**ו**	**ב**	**תָ**	**י**	**כִּ**
letter:	alef	vav	vet	tav	yod	kaf
sound:	(silent)	**Oh**	V	Tah	EE	Kee

when you enter in = KI TAVO = **כִּי תָבוֹא**

Work

The Legend

And it shall be	v'hayah	וְהָיָה
when you enter in	ki-tavo	כִּי־תָבוֹא
to the land that	el-ha-arets asher	אֶל־הָאָרֶץ אֲשֶׁר
the LORD God-your	ADONAI Eloheicha	יְהוָה אֱלֹהֶיךָ
is giving to you	noten l'cha	נֹתֵן לְךָ
as an inheritance,	na'chalah	נַחֲלָה
and you possess her	virish'tahh	וִירִשְׁתָּהּ
and you dwell in her,	v'yashavta bahh	וְיָשַׁבְתָּ בָּהּ׃
and/that you shall take	v'lakachta	וְלָקַחְתָּ
from the first of	me-reisheet	מֵרֵאשִׁית
all (the) fruit . . .	kol-p'ri	כָּל־פְּרִי

—Deuteronomy 26:1–2a

Related Words

enter!, come!	bo	בֹּא
enter into a covenant, make an agreement	ba bi-vrit	בָּא בִּבְרִית
negotiate (to enter into words with him)	ba bi-dvarim imo	בָּא בִּדְבָרִים עִמּוֹ
welcome! (blessed is the one who comes)	baruch ha-ba	בָּרוּךְ הַבָּא
next year (the year the coming)	la-shanah ha-ba'ah	לַשָּׁנָה הַבָּאָה
to be born (come to the world)	ba la-olam	בָּא לָעוֹלָם
the world to come	ha-olam ha-ba	הָעוֹלָם הַבָּא

Hit the Trail!

Entering into Prosperity

❝ **When you have come to the land ADONAI your God is giving you as your inheritance, taken possession of it and settled there; you are to take the firstfruits . . .** ❞   —*Deuteronomy 26:1–2a*

Future generations receive instructions to bring firstfruits and say, "Today I declare to ADONAI . . . I have come to the land . . . I have now brought the firstfruits . . . you, ADONAI, have given to me" (Dt. 26:3, 10).

Enter the Land, bringing firstfruits.

Tigay [p. 237] calls the mikra bikkurim (*recitation of firstfruits*) the only address to God that Torah prescribes for laity (except Dt. 21:7–8). This ritual acknowledges God's ownership of the Land. The farmer tithes one-sixtieth of his crops [M. Pe'ah 1:1]. For two years, the farmer journeys to the central Sanctuary; on the third, he sets aside firstfruits locally to benefit Levites, widows, orphans, and the ger.

The second part of the recitation recalls the life of Ya'akov: arami oved avi (*an Aramean, the wandering/ perishing one, my father*, Dt. 26:5). These words, easily memorized, recall the life of the Patriarchs, wandering in Aram, at the time God directed their steps to the Land.

? • *Read Dt. 25:19. Notice how the precondition for bringing firstfruits to the central sanctuary requires safety from enemies (safe travel, secure roads). Comment on how the portion KI TAVO (when you enter in) gives laws for the future.*

Eat Nothing Holy!

❝ *After you have separated a tenth . . . and have given it to the Levi, the foreigner, the orphan and the widow, so that they can have enough . . . you are to say . . .* ❞   —Deuteronomy 26:12–13a

The third and sixth years of the agricultural cycle require separating out tithes for defenseless members of society. Laity must stand before the kohen and state, "I have rid my house of things set aside for God and given them to the Levi, the foreigner, the orphan, and the widow" (Dt. 26:13).

Feed the defenseless, who own no land.

The declaration further states that the farmer has not eaten the ma'aser sheni (*second tithe*), which is the holy part reserved for priests to eat on holy ground in the Presence of God. Neither has the farmer eaten when tamei (*ritually impure*); nor has he eaten when in mourning; nor has he given tithe for the benefit of the dead (Dt. 26:14).

Finally, the pilgrim, who has journeyed to the place where "God will choose to have his name live" (Dt. 26:2), implores God to look down from his abode and bless his people and the (fertility of the) soil. God, not Ba'al, brings life to His Land!

? Review Dt. 26:15. Tigay [p. 244] comments that the ritual prayer requires the tithing farmer to pray—not for personal blessing, but for corporate prosperity "for your people Yisra'el." Explain the significance of this distinction.

Ascending On High

> ❝ *Today* ADONAI *your God orders you to obey these laws and rulings. Therefore, you are to observe and obey them with all your heart and all your being.* ❞
> —Deuteronomy 26:16

Thus ends the lengthy presentation of all the "laws and rulings" which Yisra'el must obey in order to become am-kadosh (*a holy people,* Dt. 26:19).

Listening to God's Voice leads to holy nationhood.

Says Moshe: et-ADONAI he'emarta lih'yot l'cha lelohim ... v'lalechet ... v'lishmor ... v'lishmo'a b'kolo (*the* LORD *you have declared to be to you God ... to walk ... to observe ... and to listen to His Voice,* Dt. 26:17). In turn, ADONAI he'emir'cha ha-yom lih'yot lo l'am s'gullah ka'asher diber-lach (*has declared you today to be to Him a most-treasured people, just as He promised you,* Dt. 26:18).

Should Yisra'el walk, obey, and listen to God's Voice, then God will elevate the nation to am-kadosh status, and raise her "high above all the nations he has made" (Dt. 26:19).

What follows from this mutual pledge of allegiance between God and His people are blessings and the prophetic words of Sefer HAD'VARIM (*the Book of Words*), culminating in the exaltation of a holy nation under God!

? *Read Dt. 26:18–19. Note the twin uses of the word "diber." God "promises" that if Isra'el walks in His ways, keeps His laws, and hearkens to His Voice, that the nation will ascend on high. Relate this picture to the experience at Sinai.*

Nationhood

> **"** *Then Moshe and all the leaders of Isra'el gave orders to the people. They said, "Observe all the mitzvot I am giving you today."* **"**
>
> —*Deuteronomy 27:1*

Christensen [p. 652] outlines this segment as a five-part structure (Dt. 27:1, 2–4, 5–7, 8, 9–10):

- v. 1 Moshe's summary command
- v. 2–4 Write Torah on Mt. Eival
- v. 5–7 Erect altar on unhewn stone
- v. 8 Write Torah on plastered stone
- v. 9–10 Moshe's summary command

Listen, obey, and become the people of God.

First, Moshe and elders order the people to observe all the commandments of this Torah (Dt. 27:1). Next, Moshe orders the people to write this Torah on plastered stones on Mt. Eival, where all Yisra'el can see the words and take them to heart (Dt. 27:2–4).

Later, the kohanim and L'vi'im declare, "Today you have become the people of Adonai your God" (Dt. 27:9). The people are told v'shamata b'kol Adonai (*you must listen to the Voice of the Lord*, Dt. 27:10).

As at Sinai, the people must cleanse, consecrate, and sanctify themselves. Then the holy ones ascend the mountain, sacrifice, fellowship in covenant, and hear the Voice of the Lord.

? Reread Dt. 27:2–3. The people must write the words of this Torah on great plastered stones at the sacrificial altar at Mount Eival. Is this the whole Torah or Sefer D'varim? Explain why the words are prominently displayed.

Covenant Renewal

" . . . *Moshe commissioned the people . . . "These are the ones who are to stand on Mount G'rizim and bless the people . . . while these are to stand on Mount 'Eival for the curse . . ."* **"**   —Dt. 27:11–13

Careful tailoring of the segment begins with instructions for a future covenant renewal ceremony in the Promised Land. The segment concludes with words of blessing, spoken in the direction of tribes standing upon the green foliage of Har G'rizim (*Mt. Gerizim*).

Blessing follows those who "enter into" covenant with God.

Buried in the middle of the segment, the Levites loudly proclaim a dozen curses upon those who make idols, dishonor parents, move neighbor's markers, or otherwise fail to uphold the words of Torah (Dt. 27:15–26).

The Levite tribe (Dt. 27:14) now assumes responsibility for speaking as the Voice of God to corporate Yisra'el (who, at Sinai, had pleaded not to hear the Voice of God directly). Tradition ascribes an oath to the people's final "amen" to the words: arur asher lo-yakim et-divrei ha-torah-ha-zot la'asot otam (*a curse on the one who does not establish the words of this Torah, to do them*), [Dt. 27:26, cf. Rashi, Shev. 36a].

? Read Dt. 27:26. Is Torah a curse for the one who does not keep it? Explain the meaning of swearing an oath on the twelfth, final curse, proclaimed by a priestly tribe to 12 tribes standing on both lush and barren ground in the Land.

Invincibility

> **"** ADONAI *will cause your enemies attacking you to be defeated before you; they will advance on you one way and flee before you seven ways.* **"**
>
> —Deuteronomy 28:7

Blessings open this segment, too, which then culminates with a summoning of all Yisra'el to seal the covenant at Mo'av with Moshe in Transjordan (Dt. 29:1(28:69‏תג"ך‎)).

Blessings for obedience, curses for disobedience.

Squeezed between these verses are the blessings of glorious national exaltation (Dt. 28:8–14) and the ever longer curses of the covenant, in the event of disobedience (Dt. 28:15–68). Called the tochehah (*warning*), these words are chanted in hushed tones by today's Torah readers. Such curses detail an erosion of independence in ever widening circles, starting with the loss of material things, then personal property, personhood, heritage holdings, and ultimately nationhood, ending tragically in service to foreign deities and imperial powers.

Truth can be too hard to swallow. Curses culminating in sieges, cannibalism, exile, and foreign domination simply overwhelm the senses.

Suppose Yisra'el chose to forget the covenant and incurred the full curse of Torah. When, then, would you expect Messiah to come? Read Dt. 28:63, cf. Is. 53:7–10. Explain bearing the burden for transgressions committed.

Eyes to See

❝ Then Moshe summoned all Isra'el and said to them, "You saw everything ADONAI did before your eyes in the land of Egypt to Pharaoh, to all his servants and to all his land . . ." ❞   —Dt. 29:2(1רבד)

Moshe summons the people, reminding them that God led them out with signs and wonders and miracles of great power. At Sinai, the people saw the thunder and the sound of the great shofar (Ex. 20:18(15רבד)). Still, the people cannot grasp the import of keeping covenant obedience and listening to God's Voice: "to this day ADONAI has not given you a heart to understand, eyes to see or ears to hear!" (Dt. 29:4(3רבד)).

Raised in the wilderness, the young generation experiences miracles as mundane events. Their clothes and shoes have never worn out, and manna comes regularly (Dt. 29:5(4רבד)). Yet all this the young have taken in stride, giving little thought to the supernatural aspect of it all.

He who has eyes to see, let him see.

Commenting on this lack of awareness, Leibowitz [pp. 292–3] detects "a note of bitter irony and deep regret in Moshe's tone . . . the sigh of disappointment" that Yisra'el still lacks "the decisive thing —the heart to appreciate" God's gifts.

? *Read Dt. 29:2–3(1–2רבד); cf. Ex. 20:19(16רבד). When did Yisra'el's "partial hardening" begin? at Sinai? after she insisted that only Moshe hear His Voice? Trace the progression of the hardening process by reading Is. 6:8–13, Ro. 11:25.*

Inheriting

" Therefore, observe the words of this covenant and obey them; so that you can make everything you do prosper. "

—Deuteronomy 29:9(8תגּ״ךּ)

The maftir concludes with a reminder that Moshe led the young generation in their miraculous victories over Sichon and 'Og, the great kings of the Transjordan vicinity. These areas become the land inheritance of the cattle-ranching firstborns, R'uven, Gad, and M'nasheh (Dt. 29:8(7תגּ״ךּ)).

> **Be fruitful, multiply, fill the Land, and subdue it.**

Thus, the maftir ends with a fitting reminder that Moshe has "entered in" to the promises as far as God permits. It remains for Y'hoshua to lead the young generation in the conquest of C'na'an.

In conclusion, Moshe urges Yisra'el to "observe the words of this covenant," so she will enter the blessings, not curses, of covenant relationship. Covenant relationship, summarized in Dt. 13:4(5תגּ״ךּ), calls Yisra'el to walk in God's ways, hold-Him-in-awe, keep His commands, hear His Voice, serve Him, and cleave to Him. Keeping these commands guarantees inheriting the Land!

? *Review Dt. 4:34–40, esp. v. 36 at Sinai. Comment on the purpose for which God hish'mi'acha et-kolo l'yas'srecha (caused you to hear His Voice in order to discipline you, Dt. 4:36).*

Days of Glory   *Meander*

> **" Arise, shine [Yerushalayim], for your light has come, the glory of ADONAI has risen over you . . . on you ADONAI will rise; over you will be seen his glory. "**
> —Isaiah 60:1–2

Light reigns in God's city, Y'rushalayim! No longer will the city need the sun by day or the moon by night, for the LORD God will be her source of light forevermore (Is. 60:20).

God personally comes to hasten Zion's glory.

God comes as Savior and Redeemer (Is. 60:16). Hopes abound as His kingdom is built. Wealth from all the nations flows to Y'rushalayim, and gold and silver replace copper and iron (Is. 60:17).

In an unwinding of curses on women, Y'rushalayim will bring forth her children without travail (Is. 60:4, 9; 66:7–9). Her citizens are tsadikim (*righteous ones*), who inherit the Land forever (Is. 60:21). In place of chamas (*lawlessness*), Y'rushalayim will call her walls Y'shu'ah (*Salvation*) and her gates T'hillah (*Praise*) (Is. 60:18).

This future comes with everlasting glory (Is. 60:2). Indeed, God closes this glorious prophecy with the promise: ani ADONAI b'itahh achishenah (*I am the LORD, in its time I will quicken it*, Is. 60:22).

? Read Is. 54:11–13, cf. Is. 60:21–22. *Explain how children personally taught by God grow to be tsadikim, the righteous. Based on the promise in Gen. 1:28, explain how righteous are blessed and grow to a thousand/to a nation.*

...ings   Firstfruits Redeemed

> **"** ...*and as he was blessing them, he withdrew from them and was carried up into heaven. They bowed in worship to him...And they spent all their time in the Temple courts, praising God.* **"** —Lk. 24:51–53

Following his death and resurrection, Yeshua appears to the disciples and opens their eyes to truths previously heard, but dismissed (Lk. 24:46–47, cf. Lk. 9:44–45, 18:31–34). Spiritual blindness does not fall away until after the resurrection!

Yeshua trumps death and enters into heaven itself.

At the ascension, Yeshua rises in the clouds of glory to the right hand of the Father in heaven. He goes up from Beit-Anyah, opposite the Mount of Olives (Lk. 24:50–52, cf. Ac. 1:9, 12). There, he instructs his disciples to wait for power from on high (Lk. 24:49, Ac. 1:8).

Speaking prophetically, the resurrection is the day of firstfruits (cf. 1 Cor. 15:20, 42–44). Believers counted the omer, not connecting the coming of the Ruach haKodesh (*Holy Spirit*) with Shavu'ot, a time when heaven and earth meet.

As Messiah ascends in the clouds, he blesses those watching. His talmidim (*disciples*) bow in worship and return to the Temple courts to praise God, giving Him glory in Y'rushalayim (Lk. 24:53).

? Read Lk. 24:46–47, cf. 9:44–45, 18:31–34. How do you cut through spiritual blindness? Read Mt. 26:6–13, Lk. 24:50–52; cf. Lev. 14:12. Explain Yeshua's ascent to heaven from the place of his anointing for burial.

Talk Your Walk . . .

KI TAVO (*when you enter in*), you inherit God's promises. Eating firstfruits continues with covenant renewal in the newly conquered lands of Mo'av. Future generations will renew the covenant in the Land of Promise itself. Obedience to Torah ensures long life in the Land, from generation to generation to the end of time.

> **Enter in to the inheritance of God!**

The Haftarah continues the sixth of seven weeks of consolation for Y'rushalayim. Redemption nears, as light and glory fill the city. God inhabits the city, granting light forevermore. The wealth of the nations flows into the city, and Y'rushalayim's own children return from afar. The righteous populate the city, to live forever within walls called "Salvation" and gates named "Praise." Glory reigns, with God's Presence returning to Y'rushalayim as Savior and Redeemer.

The B'rit Chadashah continues the theme of entering into the glorious promises of God. Messiah is resurrected as God's firstfruits from the dead. The disciples watch Yeshua ascend into the clouds of heaven. As they dutifully count the omer and praise God in the Temple courts, they fill Y'rushalayim with glory. The disciples themselves are filled with power from on high at Shavu'ot. In holy boldness, they proclaim the message of Salvation, that Yeshua has risen from the dead, for all whose eyes are opened to see.

Oasis

. . . Walk Your Talk

D o you suffer from low self-esteem? Ask the average Jewish grandfather about being "chosen." He likely will rebut your question, saying, "Ha, chosen to suffer." Yet how many are blind to the idea that apathy or disobedience to the tenets of Torah predicts the very curses of history that Jews have experienced through the ages!

Appropriating a glorious inheritance is no easy calling for a people characterized by low self-esteem. How can one overcome his self-imposed beliefs that "something must go wrong" or "I'm unworthy to be exalted over another!" Of course, no one is worthy to be exalted! But why phrase the question that way? Why not boast that

> *Boast in the LORD, and appropriate His glorious inheritance!*

God exalts those who follow Him and glory in His righteousness (Ps. 89:15–16(16–17תהִּ))?

Know that you are given not only a measure of free will in this life, but also in the time to come. Those who walk in holiness now, live more in the Ruach and less in the flesh. In so doing, they begin to live more in the glorified body of tomorrow and less in those things that are perishing today. Will you boast in God and live for Him? How can you enter into His glorious inheritance for your life?

Shabbat Shalom!

נצבים means
you ALL stand here,
alive despite curses,
so do not fear.
Love God, walk in blessings,
and you will cheer.
You CAN keep Torah,
it's very near!

Cleave to God
and not to success.
Put His Word in your heart,
survive the tests.
Hear God's Voice,
obey His requests.
He brings you back,
in the Land you shall rest!

Walk Nitsavim!
29:10(9 ‫ך‬‫"‬‫תנ‬)–30:20

‫נִצָּבִים‬

You are standing

Torah—Deuteronomy 29:10(9‫ך‬‫"‬‫תנ‬)–30:20
  1st Standing before God—Deuteronomy 29:10(9‫ך‬‫"‬‫תנ‬)
  2nd Renewing the Covenant—Deuteronomy 29:13(12‫ך‬‫"‬‫תנ‬)
  3rd Crossed Over—Deuteronomy 29:16–17(15–16‫ך‬‫"‬‫תנ‬)
  4th Blessings and Curses—Deuteronomy 30:1
  5th Repentance—Deuteronomy 30:7–8a
  6th Not Too Difficult!—Deuteronomy 30:11
  7th Choose Life—Deuteronomy 30:15, 19b
  Maftir Cleave to God—Deuteronomy 30:19b–20

Haftarah—Isaiah 61:10–63:9
  Clothed in Salvation—Isaiah 61:10

B'rit Chadashah—John 15:1–11
  The Fruitful Vineyard—John 15:11

Stand Firm . . . Choose Life!

← Looking Back

B'REISHEET (*in the beginning*), God creates a perfect paradise. But man disobeys, and God scatters him into seventy nations. Seventy SH'MOT (*names*) list sons, whom God reunites, multiplies, redeems, and calls to serve in His house as a kingdom of priests and a holy nation.

vaYIKRA ADONAI (*and the LORD called*) to Moshe from the Tent, a portable Sinai where God speaks. He instructs Yisra'el to walk in purity and minister in His dwelling. The nation surrounds God's dwelling B'MIDBAR (*in the wilderness of*) Sinai and marches out to follow the cloud on its journey to the Promised Land.

Moshe's final **D'VARIM** (*words*) exhort Yisra'el to enter the Land and appropriate her

God-given inheritance. Three sermons urge Yisra'el to obey so she can enjoy long life in the Land. Moshe recounts sins of the fathers to rally the new generation to face the giants.

In final **D'VARIM**, *Moshe says:* *"*VA'ET'CHANAN, *but you must enter the Land without me.* **EKEV** *obedience, you'll be blessed!* **R'EH**, *you can choose God's path, with* **SHOF'TIM** *for a just society."*

*"*KI TETSE—*when you go out to war, stay connected to God. Then* KI TAVO—*when you enter in, offer firstfruits to God!"*

*"*NITSAVIM—*you are standing here, to enter God's covenant. Follow Torah in your heart. Choose life!"*

Moshe reminds his people: VA'ET'CHANAN (*and I pleaded*) to enter, but God refused. The leader exhorts Yisra'el to

Log

obey Torah, lest they die in exile, too. He warns them that chosenness does not mean favoritism.

Rather, EKEV (*as a result of*) exacting obedience, God will transform the universe. R'EH (*see!*) two paths ahead: one to blessings and long life in the Land, the other path to destruction, exile, assimilation, and death. Therefore, we should appoint SHOF'TIM (*judges*), pursue justice, and cleanse the Land.

KI TETSE (*when you go out*) to war, Moshe advises, offer peace first. Maintain integrity in all relationships, especially with the vulnerable. But show no compassion to 'Amalek. Blot out evil! KI TAVO (*when you enter in*) and possess the promises, tithe on all first-fruits. Feed the needy and

In NITSAVIM . . .

The Key Person is Moshe (*Moses*), speaking to all Yisra'el (*Israel*).

The Scene is the wilderness east of the Promised Land, ready to cross over the Yarden (*Jordan*).

Main Events include <u>all</u> Yisra'el standing before ADONAI to enter His covenant; Moshe warning that idolatry will defile land and scatter people; choice between blessing and curse, life and death; God's promise to regather us; reminder that Torah is in our mouths and hearts, not too hard to obey; command to choose life and listen to God's Voice, so you and your sons will live long in the Land God promised to Avraham, Yitzchak, and Ya'akov.

those without land. Prosperity requires obedience!

Despite the curses, atem NITSAVIM (*you are standing*), this very day, on the verge of entering into the Land . . .

The Trail Ahead

The Path

אַתֶּם נִצָּבִים הַיּוֹם כֻּלְּכֶם
לִפְנֵי יהוה אֱלֹהֵיכֶם
רָאשֵׁיכֶם שִׁבְטֵיכֶם
זִקְנֵיכֶם וְשֹׁטְרֵיכֶם
כֹּל אִישׁ יִשְׂרָאֵל

—דברים כט/ט

נ	צָ	בְ	י	ם
letter:	nun	tsadee	vet	yod	mem sofeet
sound:	Nee	TtSsa	**Vee**	EE	M

you are standing = **NITSAVIM** = נִצָּבִים

Work

The Legend

You, <u>you are standing</u>	*atem <u>nitsavim</u>*	אַתֶּם נִצָּבִים
this day (lit. the day),	*ha-yom*	הַיּוֹם
all of you,	*kooll'chem*	כֻּלְּכֶם
before the face of	*lif'nei*	לִפְנֵי
the LORD God-your,	*ADONAI Eloheichem*	יְהוָֹה אֱלֹהֵיכֶם
heads-your of	*rasheichem*	רָאשֵׁיכֶם
tribes-your,	*shiv'teichem*	שִׁבְטֵיכֶם
elders-your,	*zik'neichem*	זִקְנֵיכֶם
and officers-your,	*v'shotreichem*	וְשֹׁטְרֵיכֶם
every man (of) Israel.	*kol eesh Yisra'el*	כֹּל אִישׁ יִשְׂרָאֵל:

—*Deuteronomy 29:10(9*הנ״ך*)*

Related Words

to stand, station yourself	*natsav*	נָצַב
standing, normal, perpendicular	*nitsav*	נִצָּב
pillar	*n'tsiv, matsuvah*	נְצִיב, מַצֵּבָה
station; standing place, post	*matsav*	מַצָּב
tombstone, monument, pillar, column	*matsevah*	מַצֵּבָה

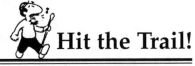

Hit the Trail!

|---|---|
| and Word Study | NITSAVIM • 141 |

Standing before God

❝ *Today you are standing, all of you, before ADONAI your God—your heads, your tribes, your leaders and your officers—all the men of Isra'el . . .* ❞
—*Deuteronomy 29:10(9 תֹּצִּ"רָךְ)*

Atem nitsavim ha-yom (*you all are standing this day*), from the greatest chief of the greatest tribe to the one with the least status, whether a woodchopper or water drawer.

Yisra'el stands to renew the covenant as the people of the LORD.

The whole nation formally presents its members to renew the covenant. Even children, women, and resident aliens take part in the covenant ceremony. The entire new generation gathers to take an "oath-of-fealty" (Fox, Dt. 29:11) to the LORD and to Him alone. This exclusive loyalty to one God sets apart Yisra'el's covenant from all other covenants in the near east [TDOT, "B'rit," pp. 253–279].

Each individual of the community must swear personal allegiance l'ov'r'cha bi-v'rit . . . u'v'alato (*to cross over into covenant . . . and into its oath-of-fealty*, Fox, Dt. 29:11). Tigay [p. 278] observes that loyalty to the covenant is guarded by imprecations, the curses read in Dt. 28. The oath alone ratifies the covenant relationship.

? *Read Dt. 29:12(11 תֹּצִּ"רָ), cf. Jer. 34:18. Rashi comments that "atem nitsavim" is best translated, "you are [still] standing," because Yisra'el had heard 49 curses in Lev. 26 and 98 curses in Dt. 28 and [still] survived. Consolatory? Explain.*

Renewing the Covenant

❝ *[The purpose is . . .] so that [A*DONAI*] can establish you today for himself as a people, and so that for you he will be God—as he said to you and as he swore to your ancestors . . .* **❞** —Dt. 29:13(12 תֹנ"ך)

generation after Sinai, God establishes the next generation in its permanent role as the people of God [Rashi]. The covenant is renewed not only with the one standing here, but also v'et asher einenu poh (*with the one who is not here,* Dt. 29:15 (14 תֹנ"ך)).

> ### *Every generation must renew the covenant.*

This covenant renewal obligates all future generations. The sages explain that all Yisra'el is standing at the renewal ceremony, and thus those "not here with us today" (Dt. 29:15(14 תֹנ"ך)) refers to the generations not yet born [Dt. 29:10(9 תֹנ"ך), Tanch. 3]. Yisra'el, not limited by time, extends the covenant across generations (cf. Dt. 5:3). Each new generation continues the story of its forebearers, including the charge for every person to renew the covenant of his fathers and mothers.

God reveals His will to exalt His people in the midst of the nations (Dt. 29:13(12 תֹנ"ך); cf. Dt. 27:9, 28:9–10, Ex. 19:5–6). Yet each generation must face the condition of blessing for obedience and curses for disobedience.

? *Read Dt. 29:15(14 תֹנ"ך), cf. Jn. 17:20–21. Note Yeshua's prayer for "those who will trust in [him] . . . that they may all be one . . . so that the world may believe." Is this prayer for yet-to-be-born generations in a timeless community? Explain.*

Crossed Over

> 66 *For you know how we lived in the land of Egypt and how we came directly through the nations you passed through; and you saw their detestable things and their idols . . .* 99 —Dt. 29:16–17(15–16ךְ"נִצ)

For a timeless community, Torah labels idolatry as "shoresh poreh rosh v'la'anah" (*a root-bearing fruit of wormwood and poison-herb,* Fox, Dt. 29:18(17ךְ"נִצ)). Thus, the sin of idolatry spreads from person to house to clan, as a poisonous branch with bitter fruit spoils a whole tree!

Maintaining the covenant determines our destiny.

The punishment for apostasy or breach of covenant is spelled out. Loss of fruitfulness eventually affects the Land, causing Yisra'elim and the nations alike to ask, "Why did ADONAI do this to the land?" (Dt. 29:22–24(21–23ךְ"נִצ)). Exile follows, "and ADONAI, in anger, fury, and incensed with indignation, uprooted them from their land and threw them out into another land—as it is today" (Dt. 29:28 (27ךְ"נִצ)).

The nations answer, "It's because they abandoned the covenant of ADONAI, the God of their fathers" (Dt. 29:25(24ךְ"נִצ)). After that, our people come to their senses. Suddenly, we realize that destiny does not depend on fate, but on keeping our covenant!

Read Dt. 29:18(17ךְ"נִצ), cf. Heb. 12:15–16. Explain how a root of bitterness causes trouble for a community. Read Dt. 29:29(28ךְ"נִצ). What responsibilities do the "revealed" things of Torah place on us and our children?

Blessings and Curses

> ❝ **When the time arrives that all these things have come upon you, both the blessing and the curse . . . then, at last, you will start thinking about what has happened to you . . . ❞**   —Deuteronomy 30:1

Moshe imparts the prophetic words: v'hayah ki-yavo'u aleicha kol-ha-d'varim ha-eleh, ha-b'rachah v'ha-k'lalah (*now it will be that when all these words/matters come upon you, the blessing and the curse,* Dt. 30:1, cf. Dt. 1:1) . . .

God's people must choose to return to God.

This post-disaster word is always read on the Shabbat just before the Ten Days of Repentance (t'shuvah, *return*). Yisra'el awakens in captivity to realize her circumstances are not fated, but rather chosen ekev (*as a result of*) her disobedience to covenant matters (Dt. 30:1). Now she will return to the LORD and listen to His Voice with a renewed commitment (Dt. 30:2; cf. Dt. 10:16).

God responds! Shav . . . et-sh'vut'cha (lit. *He returns . . . your return*), an idiom meaning that the LORD will regather Yisra'el to the Land [Dt. 30:3–5, Tigay, p. 284]. There, God circumcises the heart of Yisra'el and her children, so that she can love and obey Him even more completely (Dt. 30:6).

? *Read Dt. 30:6. Ramban writes [p. 341], "When a person seeks to purify himself, he receives help [from on high]" [Shabb. 104a]. Note how Rav Sha'ul heard God's Voice (Ac. 9), and explain God's intervention to circumcise his heart.*

Repentance

> ❝ ADONAI *your God will put all these curses on your enemies, on those who hated and persecuted you; but you will return and pay attention to what* ADONAI *says and obey . . .* ❞
> —Deuteronomy 30:7–8a

Once Yisra'el comes to her senses, God circumcises her heart (Dt. 30:1–2, 6). Wholehearted repentance becomes possible: v'atah tashuv v'shamata b'kol ADONAI v'asita et-kol-mitsvotav (*you will return, listen to God's Voice, and do all His commands,* Dt. 30:8).

Wholehearted repentance brings super-blessings!

Wholehearted repentance leads to explosive fruitfulness in offspring, livestock, and crops (Dt. 30:9, cf. 28:11). Yashuv ADONAI lasus aleicha l'tov (*the LORD will return to rejoice over you for good,* Dt. 30:9b), a stark contrast to the curse of God's taking "joy in causing you to perish and be destroyed" (Dt. 28:63).

No longer are curses of the covenant directed at Yisra'el. Punishment inflicted by one's enemies turns back upon the perpetrator.

But all these curses will reverse only if you, Yisra'el, listen to God's Voice, observe the written commandments and statutes, and turn to God b'chol-l'vav'cha oo-v'chol-nafshecha (*with all your heart and with all your soul,* Dt. 30:10).

? *Review Dt. 30:1–2, 5–6, 10, cf. Lev. 26:31, 41–42. How does God respond to "half-hearted" repentance? Explain how to progress from fatalistic attitudes, to understanding covenant consequences, to obeying, and on to full repentance.*

Not Too Difficult!

> ❝ **For this mitzvah which I am giving you today is not too hard for you, it is not beyond your reach.** ❞
> —*Deuteronomy 30:11*

Moshe states clearly that maintaining the covenant requires a wholehearted commitment to observing Torah.

> ### Torah is in your mouth, so that you can do it.

The mitsvot (*commands*) of Torah are "not too hard for you . . . [and] not beyond your reach" (Dt. 30:11). Torah's meaning is not hidden or requiring scholarly understanding. Nor is Torah to be found in some inaccessible place, such as in the heavens or the deep (Dt. 30:12–13).

"On the contrary, ki-karov ele-icha ha-davar m'od (*the word is very close to you*)—in your mouth, even in your heart; therefore, you can do it!" (Dt. 30:14).

Torah itself tells us that it is b'ficha (*in your mouth*). Says Tigay, "this manner of speaking reflects a predominantly oral culture in which learning and review are accomplished by oral recitation" [p. 286]. Talmudic sages might disparage rote memorization of Torah. Yet if Torah is in one's mouth, one knows and lives Torah by heart, even as faith establishes Torah (Ro. 3:31).

> **?** *Read Dt. 30:14, cf. 6:6–7, 31:9–13; Josh. 1:8. Chanting Torah from the scroll requires a person to internalize the vowels and trope marks. Read Eph. 5:19. Comment on the process of internalizing Torah as a love song in your heart.*

Choose Life

> **❝ Look! I am presenting you today with, on the one hand, life and good; and on the other, death and evil . . . Therefore, choose life, so that you will live, you and your descendants . . . ❞**
> —Dt. 30:15, 19b

R'eh (*see*)! The word matches the parashah that first stated the covenant blessings and curses incumbent on the people of God (cf. Dt. 11:26, see p. 70). The time has come for the new generation to renew the covenant and embrace a way of life based on the decision to choose life.

Renew the covenant! Choose blessing and long life in the Land.

With eyes wide open, the next generation is given the free will to choose its fate. On the one hand, "life and good" follow from the choice to walk in God's ways and obey His commandments; whereas, "death and evil" follow for those whose hearts turn away from God, worship foreign gods, and perish from the Land (Dt. 30:15–18).

Moshe calls "heaven and earth to witness against you today," that he has presented the choice of "life and death, the blessing and the curse" (Dt. 30:19a). He urges all Yisra'el, "Therefore, choose life, so that you will live, you and your descendants" (Dt. 30:19b). Thus ends Moshe's charge to renew the covenant.

? *Read Dt. 30:19. The everlasting witnesses to covenant renewal are heaven and earth. Why does Moshe call heaven and earth to witness "against" Yisra'el? Explain the hint that Yisra'el will fail to maintain covenant blessing.*

Cleave to God

" *Therefore, choose life . . . loving* ADONAI *your God, paying attention to what he says and clinging to him . . . On this depends the length of time you will live in the land . . .* " —Deuteronomy 30:19b–20

Cleaving to God determines "the length of time you will live in the land" (Dt. 30:20). Walking the path of blessing requires of Yisra'el: l'ahavah et-ADONAI eloheicha lish'mo'a b'kolo ul'davkah-vo (*to love the* LORD *your God, to listen to His Voice, and to cleave to Him*, Dt. 30:20).

Cleave to God and live forever!

Perfect love results in attachment. The one who loves God with wholeness of heart learns to abide in God.

Abiding in the Source of life produces vast abundance of fruitfulness. Over time, the one who abides will cleave to God. Says Sforno [p. 983], "And this will also bring you length of days to dwell on the land in this transitory life, through which you will merit everlasting life...as our sages say, 'Prepare yourself in the anteroom that you may enter the banquet hall' [Avot 4:21]."

Stern translates the concluding words well: "Therefore, choose life . . . loving ADONAI . . . and clinging to him—for that is the purpose of your life!" (Dt. 30:19–20).

? Read Dt. 30:20, cf. Jn. 15:1–18 (esp. vv. 4–5, 7–8, 10, 12, 16). Relate Yeshua's commandment of love to the concepts of abiding, cleaving, bearing fruit, and choosing life. Does cleaving to God assure Yisra'el long life in the Land? Explain.

Clothed in Salvation *Meander*

> **"** *I am so joyful in ADONAI! My soul rejoices in my God, for he has clothed me in salvation, dressed me . . . like a bridegroom wearing a festive turban, like a bride adorned with her jewels.* **"** —Isaiah 61:10

The seventh and final Haftarah, read on the Shabbat before Rosh haShanah, perfects the period of consoling Y'rushalayim. Sos asis ba'ADONAI (*I will rejoice intensely in the LORD*, Is. 61:10), sings the soul of Tsiyon.

> **"Mine eyes have seen the glory of the coming . . ."**

Tsiyon, adorned as a bride or bridegroom for a priestly wedding, comes clothed bigdei-yesha (*in garments of salvation*, Is. 61:10). Her deliverance, comfort, and renewal douse all sorrows.

God bestows new names: Tsiyon is called Cheftsi-vahh (*I delight in her*), and the Land is called B'ulah (*Espoused*) (Is. 62:4). The time comes to reverse the curse, as God swears an oath that Tsiyon's enemies will never again reap the harvests of His people (Is. 62:8–9, cf. Dt. 28:18, 44, 51, 63; 30:1–3).

God proclaims, "Your Salvation is coming" to Yisra'el, "The Holy People," and Tsiyon, the city "Sought Out" (Is. 62:11–12). Who comes? The Redeemer, majestic and speaking words of righteousness, rav l'hoshia (*mighty to save*, Is. 63:1).

? *Relate Is. 63:1 to the second blessing of the Amidah.
Note Is. 63:2–4, quoted in the "Battle Hymn of the
Republic," describes God's just dealings with enemies.
Why does the Haftarah stop just short of this glorious part?*

> ❝ *If you keep my commands, you will stay in my love—just as I have kept my Father's commands and stay in his love . . . that my joy may be in you, and your joy be complete.* ❞   —John 15:11

Scripture often likens Yisra'el to God's vineyard (e.g. Ps. 80:8–9(9–10 רֶפֶג); Is. 5:1–2, 7). Yeshua, Yisra'el's king, declares that He is the true vine (Jn. 15:1). As Gardener, the Father airei (*cuts off*) the dead wood and kathairei (*trims*) the live, to maintain a flow of life that produces fruitfulness instead of unnecessary wood (Jn. 15:2, 4).

The one who abides in the vine courses with life and bears fruit; in fact, there is no place for an unfruitful disciple (Jn. 15:5, cf. Mt. 7:20). Tenney [pp. 151–152] observes that obedience is the cause of fruitfulness, and joy is the result of fruitfulness. Bearing fruit brings glory to God (Jn. 15:8). It requires obedience and prayer to remain connected to the vine (Jn. 15:7, 10).

The connected vineyard always bears fruit.

The love which unites the Father and Son also unites us with the vine. Yeshua concludes, "I have said this to you so that my joy may be in you, and your joy be complete (Jn. 15:11).

❓ *Read Mt. 22:33–40, cf. Jn. 15:25. On which two commands did Yeshua say the whole of the Torah and Prophets depends? Explain how obeying these commands repents the sins of the fathers responsible for destroying both Temples.*

Talk Your Walk . . .

Parashat NITSAVIM shows the next generation still *"standing,"* despite the covenant curses and the dying out of the fathers in the wilderness. Only those who cleave to God escape His wrath upon the Yisra'eli men aged twenty and up. Every individual from the highest tribal chief to the lowliest water drawer assembles to renew the covenant, a personal decision that will impact the destiny of a timeless community.

> *Cleave to God, abide in the vine, and bear fruit!*

The seventh and final Haftarah of Consolation pictures God's city "forsaken" and "abandoned." Salvation nears. God will send the Redeemer to deliver His people. He renames the Land "B'ulah" (*Espoused*) and Y'rushalayim "Cheftsi-vahh" (*I delight in her*). The curse is reversed. Intense joy breaks out! The daughter of Tsiyon renews covenant relationship as "the Holy People, Redeemed of ADONAI" (Is. 62:12).

The B'rit Chadashah continues the theme of covenant blessing, with Messiah as the true vine. God's people are the vineyard, and individuals abide in the vine. Those who cleave bear much fruit, which brings great joy to the Father (pictured as the gardener, who cuts off and trims to maximize fruitfulness). Abiding in the vine requires a covenant commitment to love God, obey Torah, and pray the Father's will. God supernaturally empowers those who abide in the vine, bearing fruit and glorying in Messiah's joy.

Oasis

... Walk Your Talk

Marriage paints a picture of man in covenant relationship with God. A man leaves his father and mother's house to cleave to his wife, begin a new household, and bear children in the sacred bond of matrimony. One sees that "cleaving" is central to the mystery of how the "two become one flesh." Joy follows. Households do not age and die. Instead, they replace themselves with greater numbers of younger households. The command to "be fruitful and multiply and fill the earth" is blessed by God!

But how does man cleave directly to God? How can he know when he is cleaving and when he is not? Today, one "listens" to God's Voice by opening his inner man to hear. Purity of life and obedience to Torah help a person cleave to God.

> *Speak God's Word, and multiply His glory!*

Knowing God's will and giving it Voice is the next step. Are you open to the spiritual fact that in prayer you can know the mind of God on a particular matter (1 Cor. 2:15)? Can you "ask whatever" and then watch it happen for you? Speak God's will into creation, and He'll rejoice to answer the prayer (Jn. 15:7). Yeshua says, ". . . this is how you will prove to be my talmidim" (Jn. 15:8).

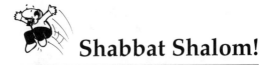

Shabbat Shalom!

וַיֵּלֶךְ means that
Moshe went
to say goodbye
at each one's tent.
He said, "Read your Torah
and always repent,
so even your children
will know what you meant."

"Now raise up Josh
to leadership.
Remember my song
when the people slip.
Tell heaven 'n earth
'bout this covenant trip,
so no one forgets
when the curses rip!"

Walk VAYELECH!
31:1–30

ויּלך

And he went

TORAH—Deuteronomy 31:1–30

HAFTARAH—Hosea 14:2–10; Joel 2:11–27; Micah 7:18–20; Isaiah 55:6–56:8
  Repent Stumbling—Hoshea 14:1–2(2–3תשו״ר)

B'RIT CHADASHAH—Romans 10:1–17
  Hear the Word!—Romans 10:16–17

Moshe Went and Y'hoshua Comes

⬅ Looking Back

B'REISHEET (*in the beginning*), God's perfect paradise crashes when man disobeys. God scatters him into seventy nations. Later, seventy **SH'MOT** (*names*) list sons whom God reunites, multiplies, redeems, and calls from Sinai to build Him an earthly dwelling.

VA**YIKRA** ADONAI (*and the LORD called*) His nation to walk in purity and minister in His dwelling, the portable Sinai where He speaks. B'**MIDBAR** (*in the wilderness*), Yisra'el surrounds God's dwelling and follows His cloud toward the Promised Land.

Moshe's prophetic **D'VARIM** (*words*) exhort Yisra'el to enter the Land! He recounts the sins of the fathers and urges the new generation to quit wandering and face the giants.

Moshe reminds his people: VA'ET'CHANAN (*and I pleaded*) with tears to enter, but God refused. He exhorts Yisra'el to obey Torah, lest they also die in exile. Yisra'el must remember that chosenness doesn't mean favoritism.

*In final **D'VARIM**, Moshe says: "VA'ET'CHANAN, but you must enter the Land without me. **EKEV** obedience, you'll be blessed! **R'EH**, you can choose God's path, with **SHOF'TIM** for a just society."*

*"**KI TETSE**, stay connected to God. **KI TAVO**, offer firstfruits to God!"*

*"**NITSAVIM**—you are standing here, to enter God's covenant. Follow Torah! Choose life!"*

*VA**YELECH**—and Moshe went to say goodbye to each tribe . . .*

Rather, **EKEV** (*as a result of*) exacting obedience, God will transform the universe. **R'EH** (*see!*), two paths lie ahead.

Log

One path leads to blessings and long life in the Land. The other leads to destruction, exile, assimilation, and death. We must choose wisely and appoint **SHOF'TIM** (*judges*) to pursue justice and keep the Land from defilement through bloodshed.

KI TETSE (*when you go out*) to war, Moshe advises, offer peace first. Maintain integrity in all relationships, especially with the vulnerable. But, to 'Amalek, show no compassion. Blot out evil! Then **KI TAVO** (*when you enter in*) and possess the promises, tithe on all firstfruits. Feed the needy and those without land.

Moshe reminds us: atem **NITSAVIM** (*you all are standing*) this very day before God! So renew the covenant, enter the Land, walk in obedience, repent wrongdoing, and

In VAYELECH . . .

The Key People are Moshe (*Moses*), speaking to all Yisra'el (*Israel*), and Y'hoshua (*Joshua*).

The Scene is the wilderness east of the Promised Land, ready to cross over the Yarden (*Jordan*).

Main Events include 120-year-old Moshe going out to continue his words for Yisra'el to be strong and of good courage; Y'hoshua's role as Yisra'el's new leader; Moshe writing down Torah to be read every seven years so all can hear and learn to obey; Moshe and Y'hoshua at the Tent of Meeting with God; the LORD telling about Moshe's death and the people's rebellion; a new song for Moshe to write down and teach as a witness against the people; command for Levites to carry the Torah in the ark; and people gathering to hear the HA'AZINU song.

cleave to God. VAYELECH Moshe (*and Moses went*) to bid each tribe farewell . . .

The Trail Ahead ➡

The Path

וַיֵּלֶךְ מֹשֶׁה וַיְדַבֵּר אֶת הַדְּבָרִים הָאֵלֶּה

אֶל כָּל יִשְׂרָאֵל וַיֹּאמֶר אֲלֵהֶם

בֶּן מֵאָה וְעֶשְׂרִים שָׁנָה אָנֹכִי הַיּוֹם

לֹא אוּכַל עוֹד לָצֵאת וְלָבוֹא

וַיהוה אָמַר אֵלַי

לֹא תַעֲבֹר אֶת הַיַּרְדֵּן הַזֶּה

‎—דברים לא/א

ךְ	לֶ	יֵּ	וַ
letter: chaf sofeet	lahmed	yod	vav
sound: CH	Leh	**Yyei**	Vah

and he went = VAYELECH = וַיֵּלֶךְ

Work

The Legend

<u>And went</u> Moses and spoke	*va-yelech* Moshe *va-y'daber*	וַיֵּלֶךְ מֹשֶׁה וַיְדַבֵּר
→ these words (lit. the words the these)	*et-ha-d'varim ha-eleh*	אֶת־הַדְּבָרִים הָאֵלֶּה
to all Israel	*el-kol-Yisra'el*	אֶל־כָּל־יִשְׂרָאֵל׃
and said to them,	*va-yomer alehem*	וַיֹּאמֶר אֲלֵהֶם
"(A) son 120 years (i.e. I am 120 years old)	*ben-meah v'esrim shanah*	בֶּן־מֵאָה וְעֶשְׂרִים שָׁנָה
I today (lit. the day).	*anochi ha-yom*	אָנֹכִי הַיּוֹם
Not am I able still	*lo-oochal od*	לֹא־אוּכַל עוֹד
to go out and to come in.	*latset v'lavo*	לָצֵאת וְלָבוֹא
And the LORD said to me,	*va-ADONAI amar elai*	וַיהוָה אָמַר אֵלַי
"Not will you cross over	*lo ta'avor*	לֹא תַעֲבֹר
→ this Jordan (lit. the Jordan the this)	*et-ha-Yarden ha-zeh*	אֶת־הַיַּרְדֵּן הַזֶּה׃

—Deuteronomy 31:1

Related Words

to go, walk, step, wander, travel, depart, disappear, vanish, pass away	*halach*	הָלַךְ
law, rule, tradition; legal part of Talmud; theory	*halachah*	הֲלָכָה
traveler	*hehlech*	הֵלֶךְ
step, walk, conduct	*halich*	הָלִיךְ
walk, journey	*mahalach*	מַהֲלָךְ
Go yourself! (Gen. 12:1)	*lech l'cha*	לֶךְ־לְךָ

to walk continuously with
   (Gen. 5:22 Enoch, Gen. 6:9 Noah,
   Gen. 17:1 Abraham)
	hit'halech	הִתְהַלֵּךְ

Hit the Trail!

Final Farewells

❝ *Moshe went and spoke the following words to all Isra'el: "I am 120 years old today. I can't get around any longer; moreover, ADONAI has said to me, 'You will not cross this Yarden.'"* ❞ —Deuteronomy 31:1–2

Moshe's one hundred and twentieth birthday commences—the last day of Moshe's life on earth [Dt. 34:7; Sot. 13b]. Moshe has lived to fullness of years (cf. Gen. 6:3). Thus, VA-YELECH Moshe (*Moses went out*) to each tribe to say his final farewells [Ibn Ezra].

He tells Yisra'el that he is no longer able latset v'lavo (*to go out and to come in*, Dt. 31:2). The contexts of two previous parashiot, KI TETSE (*when you go out*) to war and KI TAVO (*when you enter*) the Land, confirm that Moshe is no longer able to "exercise military leadership" [Tigay, p. 289].

Before passing the mantle of leadership, Moshe tells the people, "ADONAI your God—he will cross over ahead of you. He will destroy these nations ahead of you . . ." (Dt. 31:3a). God, as warrior, fights for Yisra'el. Only after first putting trust in God does Moshe mention, "Y'hoshua—he will cross over ahead, as ADONAI has said" (Dt. 31:3b).

Moshe prepares Yisra'el for his absence.

Thus, Moshe appoints Y'hoshua his successor, confirming God's word spoken to him near Beit-P'or (Dt. 3:28).

? *Read Dt. 31:3; cf. Ex. 14:14, 14:25, 15:3. Explain God's role as warrior. Offering sacrifice and prayer before battle, Yisra'el is expected to be ritually pure and obedient to God's word. Compare with spiritual warfare in Eph. 6:10–18.*

God Leads

> **❝** ADONAI *will do to them what he did to Sichon and 'Og, the kings of the Emori, and to their land—he destroyed them.* ADONAI *will defeat them ahead of you . . .* **❞**
> —Deuteronomy 31:4–5a

Recent victories cited above strengthen the people's resolve. God, who destroyed the Emori (Num. 21:21–24, 33–35), will also lead Yisra'el against the tribes in C'na'an (Dt. 31:4–5).

Keep the faith!

Chizku v'imtsu (*be strong and courageous!*, Dt. 31:6a, Josh. 1:9). God led Moshe to victory, and He will lead the people according to the mandate of Dt. 20:10–18, [Dt. 31:5, Hertz, p. 832]. Moshe comforts the people and tells them not to fear, because the LORD, hu ha-holech imach (*He is the One Who walks with you*); "He will neither fail you nor abandon you" (Dt. 31:6, Josh. 1:5, 9).

The new generation has shown faithfulness in its willingness to face Sichon and 'Og in battle. Unlike the fathers, they have not shrunk from the frightening command to face the giants of the Land. Moshe assures Yisra'el that she can be confident of victory, so long as she trusts in God's strength and not in her own (Dt. 31:6).

? Read Dt. 31:6, cf. Jd. 6:12, Jer. 1:8, 19, Mt. 28:19–20. Tigay [p. 290] comments that when God commissions someone, He promises assistance and protection. Explain how God's words strengthen those He commissions.

Be Strong and Courageous

❝...Moshe summoned Y'hoshua and, in the sight of all Isra'el, said to him, "Be strong, be bold, for you are going with this people into the land ... You will be the one causing them to inherit it." ❞ —Dt. 31:7

Moshe calls a final assembly of the people, to formally appoint Y'hoshua to leadership (Dt. 31:7; cf. Dt. 3:28). In the public ceremony, Moshe tells Y'hoshua the same words he has just told the people: "Be strong, be bold ... ADONAI ... will neither fail you nor abandon you"(Dt. 31:7–8).

Moshe appoints Y'hoshua to appropriate the Promised Land.

Y'hoshua will personally "enter" and distribute the tribal land inheritances: atah tan'chilenah otam (*you will cause them to inherit it,* Dt. 31:7; cf. Dt. 1:38). Moshe adds another twist: ADONAI hu ha-holech l'faneicha (*the LORD, He is the One Who walks <u>before</u> you,* Dt. 31:8), to establish His b'rit olam (*everlasting covenant*). Thus, God grants Avraham's seed the land of C'na'an as an everlasting inheritance (Gen. 6:9, 17:1–2, 7).

Finally, Moshe writes the sacred text and hands it to the kohanim, bearers of the ark of the covenant, and to the elders (Dt. 31:9). Now, the new guard assumes the chain of command.

? Study Dt. 31:9, 25; cf. Num. 4:15. Are kohanim and L'vi'im doing the Kohathites' job? What is the role for "all the elders" in receiving the written Torah? Read Is. 66:18b, 21; cf. 56:6–7. Does the prophet hint at a role for gentiles? Explain.

Listen to the Word

" . . . every seven years, during . . . Sukkot in the year of sh'mittah . . . in the presence of ADONAI . . . you are to read this Torah before all Isra'el, so that they can hear it. " —Deuteronomy 31:10–11

Moshe commands an assembly of Yisra'el to listen to a public reading of Torah, to take place during Sukkot miketz sheva shanim (*at the end of seven years*, Dt. 31:10).

Read Torah publicly at the end of every seventh year.

The reading commences b'mo'ed sh'nat ha-sh'mittah b'chag ha-sukkot (*at the appointed-time of the Year of Release, on the pilgrimage-festival of Sukkot*, Fox, Dt. 31:10). Tigay observes that the largest crowds went to Y'rushalayim on Sukkot. After tithing on an assured food supply, people listened to Torah with minds "free of concern" [p. 291].

At the hak'hel (*assembly*), the king would sit in the Court of Women to read. M. Sot. 7:8 reports that the king read from Dt. 1:1–6:9, 11:13–21, 14:22–29, 26:12–15, 17:14–20, 27:11–28:68, although Tigay [p. 292] says there is no reason to limit readings to the King's Lection.

Torah proclaims that this public assembly for reading Torah teaches the nation's children, at a formative time, to revere the LORD (Dt. 31:13).

In the sh'mittah year of 2001, our local congregation hosted an assembly to read Torah every evening during Sukkot. The next time for publicly reading Torah falls on day two of Sukkot in 2008. What will your city plan to do?

Write this Song

❝ ADONAI *said to Moshe, "The time is coming for you to die. Summon Y'hoshua, and present yourselves in the tent of meeting, so that I can commission him." Moshe and Y'hoshua went . . .* ❞   —Dt. 31:14

ADONAI formally commissions Y'hoshua at the Ohel Mo'ed (*Tent of Meeting*). He instructs Moshe to station Y'hoshua at the door of the Tent.

There, God appears in a pillar of cloud and speaks to Moshe: va'azavani v'hefer et-b'riti (*they will abandon Me and break My covenant*, Dt. 31:16). God's anger will "flare up" against the people for "whoring after the gods of the foreigner of the land" (Fox, Dt. 31:17, 16). The people will be beset by troubles from every side, until finally they come to their senses and ask, "Haven't these calamities come upon us because our God isn't here with us?" (Dt. 31:17).

Such a realization will not be enough; for God responds, "I, I will conceal, yes, conceal my face (*Anochi haster astir panai*) on that day, because of all the ill that they have done, for they faced-about to other gods!" (Fox, Dt. 31:18).

Commission Y'hoshua, and teach this song!

Then God directs Moshe and Y'hoshua, ". . . write this song for yourselves . . . so that this song can be a witness for me against the people of Isra'el" (Dt. 31:19).

? *Read Dt. 31:19. Observe that God instructs Moshe and Y'hoshua to write a song and teach it to the people so they "learn it by heart." What is the purpose of writing the song, and why must the people know it by heart?*

Song as a Witness

> **" For when I have brought them into the land . . . and they have eaten their fill . . . this song will testify before them as a witness . . . "**
>
> —*Deuteronomy 31:20*

Yisra'el will prosper in the Land with God's blessing. Yet the song spells out perils of prosperity.

Warning: beware the trap of prosperity in the Land.

When "they have eaten their fill, grown fat and turned to other gods, serving them and despising me, and broken my covenant . . . this song will testify before them as a witness, because their descendants will still be reciting it and will not have forgotten it" (Dt. 31:20–21). In obedience to God, Moshe writes down the song and teaches it "that same day" to the children of Yisra'el (Dt. 31:22).

Now ADONAI Himself commissions Y'hoshua, saying, "Be strong and full of courage; for you are to bring the people of Isra'el into the land about which I swore to them; and I will be with you" (Dt. 31:23). Thus Y'hoshua himself, entering Moshe's position, hears the actual Voice of God.

Finally, Moshe finishes writing all the words of this Torah al sefer ad tumam (*upon a document, until they were complete*, Dt. 31:24). Thus concludes the teaching of Torah to all the people (Dt. 31:12, 24).

> **?** Study Dt. 31:20–22. Notice that both the Torah and the song function as a "witness against" the people. Do you think that the song or the Torah becomes the last witness to restore Yisra'el to her senses? Explain your reasoning.

Torah as a Witness

> ❝ Moshe gave these orders to the L'vi'im . . . "Take this book of the Torah and put it next to the ark with the covenant of ADONAI . . . so that it can be there to witness against you." ❞
>
> —Dt. 31:25–26

Moshe charges the L'vi'im to place the sefer ha-torah ha-zeh (*the document of this Torah*) "beside" the ark, either inside the ark next to the Tablets or on a shelf [Bav. Bat. 14ab], "so that it can be there to witness against you" (Dt. 31:26).

First the Torah and now the Song witness against Yisra'el.

Christensen observes that placing the scroll as a "witness against" inaugurates a "tradition of granting a book final religious authority" [p. 781].

Moshe cites his past experience with Yisra'el, a people who have been "rebellious" and "stiff-necked . . . against ADONAI." All the more so will Yisra'el rebel under another leader's watch (Dt. 31:27).

Accordingly, Moshe calls a final assembly of leadership so he can teach them the song he has written: hak'hilu elai et-kol-ziknei shivteichem v'shotreichem (*assemble to me all of your elders and tribal officials*, Dt. 31:28). The previous assemblies at Sinai and in Mo'av hint at the importance of what follows (Dt. 4:10, 31:12).

? Read Dt. 31:26, cf. 2 Ki. 22:20–23:1. After the Babylonian exile, many people came to their senses and realized the connection between exile and violation of the covenant. Comment on the role of the public reading for opening minds.

Teach the Song

> **Then Moshe spoke in the hearing of the whole assembly of Isra'el the words of this song, from beginning to end . . .**
>
> —*Deuteronomy 31:30*

Elders and officials assembled, Moshe speaks "in their ears" that he "may call-to-witness against them the heavens and the earth" (Fox, Dt. 31:28). The maftir *concludes* with an order to internalize HA'AZINU as a prophetic witness. This song warns that Yisra'el will stumble into idolatry, break the covenant, and completely forget the consequences that come from spurning God.

Moshe summons the eternal witnesses of heaven and earth. In this way, after Moshe dies and the rest are ignorant, God will not be without a witness when He acts to enforce the covenant. God will bring misfortune upon Yisra'el for her "evil" behaviors, l'hach'iso (*vexing Him*) by worshiping foreign gods (Dt. 31:29).

Sing this song "Ha'azinu" in their ears!

All action culminates with Moshe speaking b'oznei kol-k'hal Yisra'el et-divrei ha-shi-rah ha-zot ad tumam (*in the ears of the whole assembly of Israel, the words of this song to their completion,* Dt. 31:30). The song follows next in the new portion, HA'AZINU (*give ear*)!

Talmud records that the song was sung by the L'vi'im every Shabbat at the Musaf (additional) service, in the Second Temple period [RH 31a]. Discuss the significance of making this song a regular part of the Shabbat liturgy.

Repent Stumbling *Meander*

> **" Return, Isra'el, to ADONAI your God, for your guilt has made you stumble. Take words with you, and return to ADONAI; say to him, "Forgive all guilt, and accept what is good . . ." "** — Hosea 14:1–2(2–3תהל׳)

When VAYELECH is not paired with NITSAVIM as a double portion, the reading falls on Shabbat Shuvah (*the Sabbath of Return*), also called Shabbat T'shuvah (*the Sabbath of Repentance*).

Return to God, and turn your life around.

Multiple readings make up the Haftarah section, with Ashkenazim adding from the prophet Joel and Sephardim from Micah. Reading from Hosea is universal, with its first words: Shuvah Yisra'el

(*Return, Yisra'el*)! Twice in this same verse, God implores Yisra'el to return to Him—ki chashalta ba'avonecha (*for you have stumbled in your iniquity*, Hos. 14:1(2תהל׳), cf. Ro. 11:11).

These words, read on the Shabbat before Yom Kippur, call Yisra'el to repent the life decisions that kindle wrath. God waits, saying, "I will heal their disloyalty" (Hos. 14:4(5תהל׳)). His anger turns! Granting mercy instead of judgment, God pledges to renew blessings upon the Land. Even the lost of Efrayim depart idolatry on the day Yisra'el turns and repents (Hos. 14:8(9תהל׳)).

> **?** "Forgive all guilt, and accept what is good; we will pay instead of bulls [the offerings of] our lips . . . For it is only in you that the fatherless can find mercy." How do these words from Hos. 14:2–3(3–4תהל׳) turn away God's anger?

Haftarah Hosea 14:2–10; Joel 2:11–27; Micah 7:18–20; Isaiah 55:6–56:8

> *" ... they haven't all paid attention to the Good News and obeyed ... So trust comes from what is heard, and what is heard comes through a word proclaimed about Messiah. "*   —Romans 10:16–17

The "righteousness grounded in trusting" does not say that knowing and doing Torah is impossible (Ro. 10:6–8). Rather, Torah affirms, "The word is near you, in your mouth and in your heart" (Ro. 10:8, Dt. 30:11–14).

> *The one who hears and believes can observe Torah.*

Rav Sha'ul asserts that Torah points to the message of Good News, "that if you acknowledge publicly with your mouth that Yeshua is Lord and trust in your heart that God raised him from the dead, you will be delivered" (Ro. 10:9).

Yet somehow Yisra'el has not responded. Rav Sha'ul poses several underlying questions to probe the matter. Perhaps Yisra'el hasn't trusted; maybe they didn't hear; perhaps no one has proclaimed the Good News; and maybe no one was sent (Ro. 10:14–16).

He concludes, "The problem is that they haven't all paid attention to the Good News and obeyed it" (Ro. 10:16, cf. Is. 53:1). HA'AZINU will help clarify this enigma.

> **?** *Read Ro. 10:6–8, cf. Dt. 8:17, 9:4. Explain Sha'ul's insertion, "Do not say in your heart." Does the text say that "to bring Messiah down" is God's job (not our worry); or is it telling us that Messiah, the living Word, has already come?*

Talk Your Walk . . .

VAYELECH Moshe (*and Moses went*) to bid Yisra'el farewell and make final preparations for his departure. Moshe appoints Y'hoshua as his successor, and then he sternly warns Yisra'el not to whore after foreign gods. He completes the Torah and places the scroll in the hands of the kohanim as a "witness against" Yisra'el, along with a final song to be memorized so that Yisra'el might understand that her misfortunes result from her idolatrous behaviors.

> *The covenant has terms, whether one knows them or not.*

The Haftarah reading picks up history at a time when Efrayim has fallen headlong into idolatry, suffering exile and assimilation, while Yisra'el suffers the yoke of foreign domination. Through the prophet, God calls his people to come to their senses, turn, and repent idolatry.

The B'rit Chadashah reading describes Y'hudah, now named Yisra'el, suffering under the yoke of the Roman Empire. Rav Sha'ul asks why Yisra'el has failed to repent such oppressive circumstances. Each question leads to another: why hasn't Yisra'el trusted? didn't Yisra'el hear? has no one told them? did God fail to send a messenger? With no obvious failures in the chain, Rav Sha'ul concludes that Yisra'el has failed to pay attention. Failure to obey the terms of the covenant sows Roman occupation and hardships designed to awaken Yisra'el to cry out to the LORD for deliverance from the oppressor.

Oasis

. . . Walk Your Talk

No one is as blind as the man who will not see! By extension, no one is as deaf as he who will not hear. Have you ever met a person who put his hands over his ears and tells you, "Don't convince me with the facts, my mind is made up!"

Our generation is not all that keen to teach Torah to the bar/bat mitzvah generation. Somehow the formalities of the party get more attention than the meaning of the d'rash or the learning of trope.

Not many people value reading or chanting Torah for its own sake. Nor is bar mitzvah training directed toward equipping a child to develop a sustainable life habit of reading and singing other portions (or all portions) for oneself. Simply put, to nurture oneself on the "meat" of God's Word is not in style.

Yet Moshe commanded Yisra'el to impart Torah as an everlasting heritage across generations. And he knew full well that Yisra'el would fall short, whore after foreign gods, and be expelled—to die in exile as Moshe himself

> ### *Learn HA'AZINU as a song in your heart!*

was experiencing! So he summarized all of Torah in a song to be learned by heart long after Torah was no longer taught. Moshe ordered this song to be "put in your ears." Will you *"give ear"* to learn HA'AZINU??

Shabbat Shalom!

הַאֲזִינוּ means
to my song, "Give ear!"
If you love other gods,
you shall live in fear.
You'll wind up in exile
with nothing to cheer,
and I'll hide from you.
I will not draw near!
Be careful with riches
inside the Land.
Abe's family may be
more numerous than sand,
but don't think it's you
who makes life grand.
A L L blessings flow
from the strength of <u>MY</u> hand!

Walk Ha'azinu!
32:1–52

Give ear!

TORAH—Deuteronomy 32:1–52

HAFTARAH—2 Samuel 22:1–51

B'RIT CHADASHAH—Romans 10:17–11:12, 12:19, 15:9–10

Give Ear!
God Demands Exclusive Loyalty

⬅ Looking Back

B'REISHEET (*in the beginning*), God creates paradise, but man disobeys and gets scattered into seventy nations. Seventy SH'MOT (*names*) list sons whom God reunites, multiplies, redeems, and calls to His House as a kingdom of priests and a holy nation.

VAYIKRA ADONAI (*and the LORD called*) to Moshe from His dwelling, the portable Sinai where He speaks. B'MIDBAR (*in the wilderness*), Yisra'el surrounds God's dwelling and follows God's cloud to the Promised Land.

In Sefer **D'VARIM** (*the Book of Words*), Moshe exhorts Yisra'el to enter the Land. Moshe reminds his people: VA'ET'CHANAN (*and I pleaded*) with tears to enter, but God refused. Moshe exhorts Yisra'el to obey Torah, lest they die in exile, too. He warns Yisra'el that chosenness

does not merit favoritism. Rather, EKEV (*as a result of*) their exacting obedience, God will transform the universe.

In final **D'VARIM**, *Moshe says:*
*"*VA'ET'CHANAN, *but I may not enter the Land with you.*
EKEV *obedience, be blessed!*
R'EH *God's path, and choose*
SHOF'TIM *to keep justice."*

*"*KI TETSE, *stay connected to God.*
KI TAVO, *offer firstfruits!*
All of you NITSAVIM *before God.*
Follow Him!"

VAYELECH *Moshe to tell each tribe goodbye.*
Then he taught us a song . . .
*"*HA'AZINU! *Give ear!"*

R'EH (*see!*), two paths lie ahead. One path leads to blessings and long life in the Land, the other to curses and a DEAD end—destruction, exile, assimilation, and death. Therefore, appoint SHOF'TIM

Log

(*judges*) to pursue justice and redeem the Land.

KI TETSE (*when you go out*) to war, Moshe says to offer peace first. Maintain integrity in relationships, but blot out 'Amalek forever! KI TAVO (*when you enter in*) and possess the promises, tithe on all firstfruits. Feed the needy and those without land.

Remember, despite the curses, that you still NITSAVIM (*are standing*) this very day, overlooking the Land. Therefore, renew the covenant, enter the Land, walk in obedience, repent any wrongdoing, and cleave to God! VAYELECH Moshe (*and Moses went out*) on his last day on earth, to bid farewell. He appoints Y'hoshua to succeed him and exhorts Yisra'el to read Torah every seven years, so her children will learn to fear God. Finally, Moshe teaches a song which summa-

In HA'AZINU . . .

The Key People are Moshe (*Moses*) and Y'hoshua (*Joshua*), speaking to all Yisra'el (*Israel*).

The Scenes are the wilderness east of the Promised Land, and Har N'vo (*Mt. Nebo*) with its view of the Land across the Yarden (*Jordan*).

Main Events include Moshe and Y'hoshua reciting the HA'AZINU song to all the people gathered; song used as a teaching poem, calling heaven and earth to "give ear" as witnesses of Yisra'el's disobedience, which leads to devastation and dispersion but eventual regathering; later the same day, Moshe climbing Mt. Nebo to view the Promised Land before dying.

rizes history and reminds Yisra'el to come to her senses when she breaks the covenant and incurs judgment.

The song begins: HA'AZINU (*give ear!*) that God is just and faithful to keep His covenant forever . . .

The Trail Ahead ➡

The Path

האזינו השמים ואדברה

ותשמע הארץ אמרי פי

—דברים לב/א

ו	נ	י	ז	אֶ	הַ
letter:	vav	nun	yod	zayin	alef	hay
sound:	OO	N	EE	**Zee**	(silent)-ah	Hah

give ear! = **HA'AZINU** = **הַאֲזִינוּ**

Work

The Legend

<u>Give ear,</u>	*ha'azinu*	הַאֲזִינוּ
the (i.e. oh) heavens,	*ha-shamayim*	הַשָּׁמַיִם
and I will speak,	*va-adaberah*	וַאֲדַבֵּרָה
and may hear	*v'tish'ma*	וְתִשְׁמַע
the earth	*ha-arets*	הָאָרֶץ
(the) sayings of mouth-My.	*imrei-fee*	אִמְרֵי־פִי׃

—Deuteronomy 32:1

Related Words

listen, give ear	*azan*	אָזַן
ear/hearing, ears (pl.)	*ozen, oznayim*	אֹזֶן, אָזְנַיִם
to listen to the radio	*he'ezin l'radio*	הֶאֱזִין לְרַדְיוֹ
headphone	*aznit rosh*	אָזְנִית רֹאשׁ

ears they have
  but hear not
Hamantasch(en)
  (Purim cookies shaped
  like Haman's hat or ear)
	oznayim lahem
	v'lo yishma'oo
	ozen Haman,
	oznei Haman (pl.)
		אָזְנַיִם לָהֶם
		וְלֹא יִשְׁמָעוּ
		אֹזֶן הָמָן,
		אָזְנֵי הָמָן

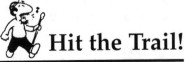

Hit the Trail!

Call Witnesses

> **" Hear, oh heavens, as I speak!**
> **Listen, earth, to the words from my mouth! "**

—*Deuteronomy 32:1*

The song of Moshe follows an ancient literary form, sometimes called a rib-pattern (after riv, Hebrew for *lawsuit*). Suzerains used this type of poetry to confront their wayward vassals.

God states His case against His people.

The song summons heaven to give hear (and earth to reflect) God's case against His rebellious covenant partner, Yisra'el. Moshe hopes the teachings of this lengthy, didactic poem will "fall like rain ... condense like dew" into the hearts of the new generation (Dt. 32:2).

Moshe proclaims God's greatness—the Tsur (*Rock*), whose "work is perfect," tsadik v'yashar hu (*righteous and straight is He*, Dt. 32:4). So great a God and so tamim (*perfect*) in His ways, who could imagine His children as "a crooked and perverted generation ... so lacking in wisdom" (Dt, 32:5–6a)? It is all the more astounding, since God is the Father and Creator who formed and prepared His people, Yisra'el (Dt. 32:6).

? *Read Dt. 32:4–6. Whom does God call "am naval" (foolish people)? God is the "Rock." His word never changes.*
● *Being "righteous and straight," God rewards measure for measure. But how does Yisra'el repay her Father and Creator?*

Recall Mighty Acts

> **"** *Remember how the old days were;*
> *think of the years through all the ages.*
> *Ask your father—he will tell you;*
> *your leaders too—they will inform you.* **"**
> —*Deuteronomy 32:7*

As Father and Creator, the LORD directs Yisra'el to listen to their elders' stories about the genesis of mankind (Dt. 32:7–9). They speak of the days of Noach, when the Most High spread out the human race and established boundaries for the seventy sons who matured into the nations of the world; how ADONAI reserved Ya'akov alone for "his allotted heritage."

The story speeds on to find Yisra'el cast out by Pharaoh and isolated, unformed and unprotected "in a howling, wasted wilderness"

(Dt. 32:10a). God surrounded Yisra'el, cared for him, and protected him "like the pupil of his eye" (Dt. 32:10b). Then, as an eagle "arousing its nest, hovering over its young, spreading its wings . . . carrying them," so did God raise Yisra'el and teach him to soar (JPS, Dt. 32:11).

God redeemed slaves and elevated them to oversee His creation.

The section concludes that God alone raised Yisra'el to sonship, and "no alien god was with Him" (Dt. 32:12).

?• *Read Dt. 32:10–12. Watching eagles train, Bent, p. 797, says, ". . . roughly handling the youngster, [the mother] allowed him to drop . . . 90 feet; then she would swoop down . . . wings spread, and he would alight . . . " Comment.*

Prosperity Problems

> ❝ *He made them ride on the heights of the earth.*
> *They ate the produce of the fields.*
> *He had them suck honey from the rocks*
> *and olive oil from the crags . . .* ❞
> —Deuteronomy 32:13

Soaring over the highest places on earth, the eagle teaches its young ones the fun of adventure. The young suckle on "honey from the rocks and olive oil from the crags" (Dt. 32:13).

enav tishteh-chamer (*blood of grapes, you drank fermented*, Dt. 32:14e). In this five-part stanza, the song reverses, spiraling downward for 25 verses, until righting itself in Dt. 32:39, the other five-part stanza.

Y'shurun grows fat . . .   *then gross!*
He spurns God . . .   *to serve new gods*
your fathers never knew   *—Dt. 32:15–17*

The growing eagle would drink "curds from the cows and milk from the sheep" in the Land of milk and honey (Dt. 32:14). Growing stronger still, he feasts on luxurious lamb fats and the finest flour. Finally, as an adolescent, dam-

Y'shurun (*Little Straight One*)—shamanta, avita, casita (*you grew fat, thick, gross*)! You sacrificed to non-gods, johnnys-come-lately. "You ignored the Rock who fathered you, you forgot God, who gave you birth" (Dt. 32:18).

? *Read Dt. 32:15–18. Explain how this indictment of Yisra'el warns about dangers of prosperity. Are affluent societies vulnerable to the "blessings of prosperity?" How can you enjoy God's blessings and avoid the snares?*

God Provoked

> " *ADONAI saw and was filled with scorn at his sons' and daughters' provocation.* "

—*Deuteronomy 32:19*

Reacting to Yisra'el's whoremongering with anger and disgust, the LORD exclaims: astirah fanai meihem, ereh mah acharitam (*I will hide My face from them, I will see what will be their later experience*, Dt. 32:20). God concludes that it is a "twisted" generation—lo-emun bam (*there is no faith in them*, Dt. 32:20).

Yisra'el's faithlessness triggers a loud outcry from God Himself: Hem kin'uni v'lo-el/kiasuni b'havleihem v'ani akniem b'lo-am/b'goi naval achisem (*They made Me red-faced with a no-god/angered*

Me with their transitoriness so I will make them red-faced with a no-people/with a nation of fools I will anger them, Dt. 32:21; cf. Ro. 10:19).

Angered and disgusted, God hides His face, withdraws His protection.

God's mercy turns to strict justice, kindling fires of wrath: crops afire, famine, plague, pestilence, beasts, and fiery venom (Dt. 32:22–25). Then, cruel armies attack; but neither Yisra'el nor its enemies discern the power of God at work!

? *Explain why God considered, but rejected, blotting out all memory of Yisra'el (Dt. 32:26). Why would God "fear" misperceptions of the enemy—that their hand is raised high, and God has not worked all this (Dt. 32:27)?*

No Discernment

" If they were wise they could figure it out and understand their destiny. "

—*Deuteronomy 32:29*

Victors, whether historical Yisra'el or gentiles used as God's instrument, fail to discern the power of God at work. They wrongly credit their own power.

Everyone lacks wisdom.

A perilous, but constructive, ambiguity is at work. The victors do not ask, "How can one chase a thousand and two put ten thousand to rout?" (Dt. 32:30). The song even answers the unasked question: "For our enemies have no rock like our Rock—even they can see that!" (Dt. 32:31). Ironically, Yisra'el is so intent on being like the nations that she cannot see that God is the only Rock!

The ambiguity continues. The Land produces vines like those from S'dom, with poisonous grapes and clusters of gall (Dt. 32:32). God awaits the loss of His people's strength (Dt. 32:36). When all is lost, He will ask, "Where are their gods, the rock whom they trusted? Who ate the fat of their sacrifices and drank the wine of their drink offering?" (Dt. 32:37–38).

? *Read Dt. 32:32; cf. Is. 53:10–12, Jn. 19:28–30. Explain how the Land, reflecting the choices of man, produces poisonous fruits and clusters of gall. Why does Yeshua say he is thirsty? Does drinking sour wine relate to bearing sins?*

Vindication

> **" For I lift up my hand to heaven and swear,**
> **"As surely as I am alive forever, . . .**
> **I will render vengeance to my foes,**
> **repay those who hate me." "**
> **—Deuteronomy 32:40–41**

A space partitions each verse as the poetry flows with blessing across two columns, read in Hebrew from right to left. When Dt. 32:14 ends mid-column, the pattern of curses shifts to reading the left half-line for each verse first, then spiraling down half-line by half-line. Finally in Dt. 32:40, the right-to-left pattern of blessing resumes to conclude the song.

God vows vengeance on those who hate Him. The term "nakam" squares accounts for justice owed. Better translated as *defensive vindication* (NAV, Dt. 32:41), nakam lacks connotations of *revenge*.

What goes around, comes around. By punishing Yisra'el too severely, her enemies incur swift judgment themselves: "I will make my arrows drunk with blood, my sword will devour flesh . . . me-rosh par'ot oyev (*from the head of the leaders of the enemy*)" (Dt. 32:42).

God imposes justice, repaying nations measure for measure.

God turns His wrath upon zealots who go too far. Moshe charges, "Sing out, you nations [with] his people . . . he will render vengeance . . . and make atonement for the land of his people" (Dt. 32:43).

> **?** Read Dt. 32:42–43. Explain why God focuses punishment on the head zealots of the enemies of Yisra'el. Note that God's vindication "atones" for "the land of his people." How does the shed blood of the enemies atone for the Land?

Transmit the Song

> **" Moshe came and proclaimed all the words of this song in the hearing of the people and of Hoshea the son of Nun. "**
>
> —Deuteronomy 32:44

Thus, Moshe proclaims this song b'oznei ha-am (*in the ears of the people*, Dt. 32:44). Says Abarbanel, Moshe teaches the song three times: to those around him, to the elders, and to the nation (Dt. 31:22, 28, 30).

Yisra'el learns the song.

Moshe and Hoshea (i.e. Y'hoshua) stand together, though only Moshe teaches the song [Rashi]. Once again, Moshe chides Yisra'el with the words, "Take to heart all the words" asher anochi me'id bachem ha-yom (*which I testify against you this day*) asher t'tsavum et-b'neichem (*which you are to command your children*, Dt. 32:46).

Moshe reminds Yisra'el a final time that the song is a witness against them in the time to come. They must instruct their children to take this song to heart, so that its warning is never lost or forgotten.

Thus, Yisra'el is called to master Torah, ki lo-davar rek hu mi-kem (*because not an empty word is it for you*, Dt. 32:47a). Rather, "through it you will live long in the land" (Dt. 32:47b).

? Stone [p. 1111] says, "The Song does not make the future redemption conditional upon repentance; rather, it guarantees our survival and the downfall of our enemies." Can Yisra'el behold Messiah, then repent? (See Zech. 12:10–14.)

See from Afar

> **So you will see the land from a distance, but you will not enter the land I am giving to the people of Isra'el.**
>
> —Deuteronomy 32:52

To summarize the movement of the parashah, God orders Moshe to ascend to the peak of Har N'vo (*Mt. Nebo*) and to look across Y'recho into all the land of C'na'an.

Moshe sees, but cannot grasp, the glory of the promises.

God tells Moshe, ". . . you broke faith with me there among the people of Isra'el at the M'rivat-Kadesh [*Striving of Holiness*] Spring" (Dt. 32:51). He states the reason: lo-kidashtem oti (*you did not sanctify Me*) in the midst of Yisra'el (Dt. 32:51, cf. Num. 20:1–13). As a consequence, Moshe "will see the land from a distance," v'shamah lo tavo (*but to there, you shall not enter,* Dt. 32:52). Thus, Moshe, as corporate head of the nation, sees the promises only from afar. He dies with all the fathers in exile, as it were, outside the Land.

The witness of the song testifies, ironically so, against Moshe himself. Yet as Moshe falls short of the glory of God, he imparts the song to bless Yisra'el with knowledge that God guarantees the covenant!

? *The parashah has 20+30+2 verses (כל"ב), a mnemonic for kluv (basket), "the culmination of the covenant, which prevents us from ever forgetting the Torah. Or, it may allude to Caleb, who remained loyal ..." [Stone, p. 1111]. Discuss.*

David's Song   *Meander*

> ❝ So I give thanks to you, ADONAI, among the nations;
> I sing praises to your name.   He is a tower of salvation
> for his king;   he displays grace   to his anointed,
> to David and his descendants   forever. ❞
> —2 Samuel 22:50–51

Shirat David (*the song of David*) celebrates God's blessings and rewards for faithful service and obedience. David sings that God is his Tsur (*Rock,* 2 Sam. 22:3, 32, 47) whose ways are tamim (*perfect,* 2 Sam. 22:24, 26, 33).

> ### David celebrates the victories of covenant blessing.

David composed this song in his early years. He kept it close by, "reciting it on every occasion of personal salvation [Abarbanel in Stone, p. 1205]. These times included life-

threatening situations when being hunted by King Sha'ul (*Saul*) and later when at war with his enemies. David concludes by crediting God with being the Rock, Who graces him with an everlasting dynasty (2 Sam. 22:47, 51).

David cries, "Exalted be God, the Rock of my salvation . . . who gives me nakam (*vengeance*) . . . you rescue me from men of chamas (*violence*) . . . So I give thanks to you, ADONAI, among the nations" (2 Sam. 22:47–50). Both HA'AZINU and Shirat David close on this note of worldwide praise.

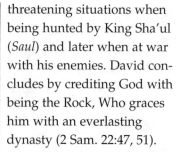

? Note the pattern of each song as written in the Hebrew. HA'AZINU (*a song of prophetic warning*) is brick-on-brick, whereas Shirat David (*a victory song*) is brick-on-half-brick [T.Y. Meg. 3:7]. Which structure seems more stable?

> **"** . . . *as it is written in the Tanakh, "Because of this I will acknowledge you among the Gentiles and sing praise to your name." And again it says, "Gentiles, rejoice with his people."* **"**
>
> —**Romans 15:9–10**

Rav Sha'ul weaves key provisions of HA'AZINU through the latter part of Romans and concludes with back-to-back closing verses from the songs of David and Moshe (Ro. 15:9–10, cf. 2 Sam. 22:50, Dt. 32:43).

Sha'ul wonders if Yisra'el understood the Good News concerning Messiah's victory over death (Ro. 10:16–18). He answers his question by quoting HA'AZINU, that God calls non-nations to know what Yisra'el fails to understand (Ro. 10:19, cf. Dt. 32:21). Though a chosen remnant knows, the majority "have been made stonelike" (Ro.

11:7–8, cf. Dt. 29:4(3תדר), Is. 29:10).

Yisra'el stumbles, but a greater glory is promised from afar.

Sha'ul asks if Yisra'el has stumbled so as to "have permanently fallen away" (Ro. 11:11). Heaven forbid! Rather, God intentionally provokes Yisra'el to jealousy (Ro. 11:14, note Dt. 32:21).

Nakam (*vengeance without revenge*) belongs solely to God—He will repay (Dt. 32:35, 40-42; cf. Ro. 12:19). When God judges, all nations will sing His praises (Ro. 15:9–10).

? *Read Ro. 11:12, 25–26. What is the purpose of the "partial hardening" of Yisra'el? When and how is this corporate hardening removed? Relate Ro. 15:9–10 (quoting 2 Sam. 22:50 and Dt. 32:43) to "the fullness of the gentiles."*

Talk Your Walk . . .

Parashat HA'AZINU summarizes how God created the nations—including Yisra'el, His "allotted inheritance." The song, written to be internalized by Yisra'el and her children, witnesses God's gracious provision and Yisra'el's twisted response. Disgusted and provoked, God "turns His face" and withdraws His protection. Only after ruthless enemies crush Yisra'el too severely, will God vindicate His people and restore justice. The nations will sing God's praises when He atones for the Land of His people.

The Haftarah, Shirat David (*the Song of David*), celebrates the justice of God against David's enemies. In contrast to unfaithful Yisra'el of HA'AZINU, David experiences the blessings of covenant faithfulness. By remembering God's past provision, the song glorifies God as the Rock, whose ways are perfect. God, in turn, rescues David from men of chamas (*lawlessness*); and David sings God's praises among the nations.

> *God's blessings and wrath will turn all the nations to sing His praises.*

The B'rit Chadashah explains how Yisra'el is partially hardened by God, a key factor being that she has spurned the Messiah. God opens the eyes of the Gentiles to sing His praises among the nations. But those who come to annihilate Yisra'el will face the justice of God, because He will send the Redeemer to deliver His people. In this way, God redeems Yisra'el's stumbling and completes His work among the nations.

Oasis

. . . Walk Your Talk

Does anyone comprehend the whole of God's work? So many unanswered questions, surely none of us sees more than part of the picture. To the other parts, we are blind or, in some cases, hardened. God must circumcise the hardened heart.

Sin twists, perverts, and eventually blinds. No one is as blind as he who will not see. Beware of willful decisions to harden! The results take on a life of their own. Prejudices, stereotypes, hatreds, and twisted ways get passed on without thought. It takes an act of God to bring healing; and it takes a wholehearted effort to prevent lapsing into familiar ways and comfortable patterns of past behaviors.

Do you have a spiritual blindness? Could you sing God's praises if you thought He were unfair? Suppose God takes both Jews and Gentiles to sing praises in His Temple. Will you write the words of HA'AZINU as a song in

> *Prepare now to sing His praises!*

your heart? Will you sing His praises today?

"Great and wonderful are thy wondrous deeds,

O Lord God, the Almighty,

Just and true are all thy ways, O Lord,

King of the ages art Thou . . ." [Dauermann, from Rev. 15:3]

Shabbat Shalom!

וזאת הברכה
means, "This is the blessing"
that Moshe gave
to the tribes who were dressing
for war with C'na'an—
a matter so pressing
that even the Canaanites
thought it was stressing!

He blessed the Levites
to be Isra'el's priest
and asked for Yosef
a terrific increase.
To all tribes he promised
some land and a feast.
Of all prophets, Moshe was
greatest—not least!!

Walk v'Zot haB'rachah!
33:1–34:12

וְזֹאת הַבְּרָכָה

And this the blessing

Torah—Deuteronomy 33:1–34:12
- 1st Blessing from Moshe—Deuteronomy 33:1
- 2nd Blessing the Priesthood—Deuteronomy 33:8
- 3rd Blessing the Land—Deuteronomy 33:13
- 4th Blessing Torah Study—Deuteronomy 33:18
- 5th Blessing the Water Supply—Deuteronomy 33:22
- Chatan Torah Groom of the Torah—Deuteronomy 33:27
- Chatan b'Reisheet Groom of New Beginnings—Genesis 1:1
- Maftir Fulfilling All of the Torah—Numbers 29:35–36a

Haftarah—Joshua 1:1–18
- Y'hoshua Succeeds Moshe—Joshua 1:1–2

B'rit Chadashah—Revelation 21:9–22:5
- Yeshua Succeeds Y'hoshua—Revelation 22:5

Rest in the Promised Land— This Is the Blessing!

Hiker's

Looking Back

Moshe's prophetic **D'VARIM** (*words*) prepare us to enter the Land God promised to the Fathers in times long ago. Ironically, the present generation of fathers has disobeyed God's direct commands. They incurred God's curse and died in the wilderness. Even Moshe must die!

VA'ET'CHANAN (*and I pleaded*) to enter the Land, he tells us. But God answered, "Enough for you!" Only those who hear God's Voice and obey will walk in His highest blessings. Yet some hope remains. **EKEV** (*as a result of*) our exacting obedience, God will open a way to long life in the Land. In fact, even nature will glory in God's purposes and cause God's enemies to flee. **R'EH** (*see*)! One path leads to blessing and life in the Land, with

Moshe's final **D'VARIM** *say:*
*"***VA'ET'CHANAN,*** but only you shall enter the Land.*
EKEV *obedience, be blessed!*
R'EH *God's path. Choose*
SHOF'TIM *to keep justice."*

*"***KI TETSE,*** stay connected to God.*
KI TAVO, *offer firstfruits!*
NITSAVIM *before God.*
Live for Him!"

VAYELECH *Moshe to say goodbye.*
Then he taught us a song.
*"***HA'AZINU!*** Give ear!"*
V'ZOT HAB'RACHAH—*and this is the blessing!*

peace and secure borders. The other path leads to curses and a DEAD end (destruction, exile, assimilation, and death of the nation).

Moshe commands us to appoint **SHOF'TIM** (*judges*) to ensure a just society and keep the Land free from bloodshed. He continues: **KI TETSE** (*when you go out*) to war, offer peace

---

Log

first, but show no compassion to those who fight you. **KI TAVO** (*when you enter in*) to the Land, rejoice in your inheritance and re-new the covenant across generations. Atem **NITSAVIM** (*you all are [still] standing*) here today, despite the curses that struck down your fathers, because God swore that Avraham's seed will one day inherit His promise.

VA**YELECH** Moshe (*and Moses went out*) to bid each tribe goodbye. Knowing future generations would forsake the covenant, Moshe teaches a song that explains how God decides to bless or curse His people.

HA**'AZINU** (*give ear*) to this song! Sing it in every generation, so that you will know God blesses the obedient and pays back, measure for measure, those who oppose Him. V**'ZOT HAB'RACHAH** (*and this is*

In V'ZOT HAB'RACHAH . . .

The Key People are Moshe (*Moses*), blessing the twelve tribes, and Y'hoshua (*Joshua*).

The Scene is the climb from the plains of Mo'av (*Moab*) up to Har N'vo (*Mt. Nebo*) in the Pisgah mountain range east of Y'recho (*Jericho*), viewing all of the Promised Land.

Main Events include Moshe blessing each tribe, then climbing Mt. Nebo to view the Promised Land; Moshe's death at age 120, burial in Mo'av by the LORD; Israelites mourning for 30 days; Y'hoshua filled with the spirit of wisdom, ordained to leadership; and a tribute to Moshe as the only prophet who spoke with God face-to-face.

---

the blessing) upon the tribes: God recreates things anew as B**'REISHEET** (*in the beginning*) . . . The new heavens and the new earth will descend, and man will eat from the tree of life!

The Trail Ahead

The Path

וְזֹאת הַבְּרָכָה
אֲשֶׁר בֵּרַךְ מֹשֶׁה
אִישׁ הָאֱלֹהִים
אֶת בְּנֵי יִשְׂרָאֵל
לִפְנֵי מוֹתוֹ

—דברים לג/א

	ת	**א**	**זֹ**	**וְ**
letter:	tav	alef	zayin	vav
sound:	T	(silent)	**Zo**	V'

	ה	**כַ**	**רַ**	**בְּ**	**הַ**
letter:	hay	chaf	reish	bet	hay
sound:	H	**CHah**	Rah	B'	Hah

and this		**v'Zot**		**וְזֹאת**
the blessing	=	**hab'rachah**	=	**הַבְּרָכָה**

Work

The Legend

And this (is)	*v'zot*	וְזֹאת
the blessing	*ha-b'rachah*	הַבְּרָכָה
that	*asher*	אֲשֶׁר
blessed Moses,	*berach Moshe*	בֵּרַךְ מֹשֶׁה
man of God,	*eesh ha-Elohim*	אִישׁ הָאֱלֹהִים
→ (the) sons of Israel	*et-b'nei Yisra'el*	אֶת־בְּנֵי יִשְׂרָאֵל
before death-his.	*lif'nei moto*	לִפְנֵי מוֹתוֹ:

—*Deuteronomy 33:1*

Related Words

and this is the Torah	*v'zot ha-Torah*	וְזֹאת הַתּוֹרָה
the Lord bless you	*y'varekh'cha Adonai*	יְבָרֶכְךָ ה'
God, blessed be He	*haShem yitbarach*	הַשֵּׁם יִתְבָּרַךְ
Thank God! (blessed is the name)	*baruch haShem*	בָּרוּךְ הַשֵּׁם
welcome (blessed is the one who comes)	*baruch ha-ba*	בָּרוּךְ הַבָּא
blessed is the Lord who is blessed	*bar'choo et Adonai ha-m'vorach*	בָּרְכוּ אֶת יְיָ הַמְבֹרָךְ
priestly benediction	*birkat kohanim*	בִּרְכַּת כֹּהֲנִים
toast (cup of blessing)	*kos shel b'rachah*	כּוֹס שֶׁל בְּרָכָה

Hit the Trail!

Blessing from Moshe

> ❝ *This is the blessing that Moshe, the man of God, spoke over the people of Isra'el before his death ...* ❞
>
> —Deuteronomy 33:1

Both the first and last books of Torah end with a dying man blessing the sons of Yisra'el. In Sefer B'REISHEET, Ya'akov blesses his sons; now in Sefer D'VARIM, Moshe blesses the tribes that descended from those sons.

In the end, the blessings triumph over the curses.

Both blessings concern themselves with the names of the sons and tribes. These names generate a unique calling for each son, as well as directions for the "future development of each tribe within the covenant nation" [Keil and Delitzsch, p. 494].

Moshe acknowledges the unity of the twelve, who enter the covenant and accept the LORD as king of Y'shurun (*Little Straight One*, idealized Yisra'el, Dt. 33:2–5). He then turns to bless each tribe individually.

Though R'uven has lost the birthright, his tribe still gets blessed first (Dt. 33:6, cf. Gen. 49:3–4). Next, Moshe blesses the tribe of Y'hudah and affirms his status as leader of armies (Dt. 33:7; cf. Gen. 49:8–10, Jd. 1:1–2).

> ❓ *Read Dt. 32:50–33:1. Notice the abrupt change from heavy criticism by Moshe in Dt. 32 to favorable treatment of the tribes inheriting blessings in Dt. 33. Explain why R'uven is blessed first, despite his sin in Gen. 35:22.*

Blessing the Priesthood

> ❝ *Of Levi he said: "Let your tumim and urim be with your pious one, whom you tested at Massah, with whom you struggled at M'rivah Spring."* ❞
> —*Deuteronomy 33:8*

From Moshe, Levi inherits priestly blessings for observing God's Word and safeguarding His covenant (Dt. 33:9). Not mentioned are Levi's vile deeds with Shim'on at Sh'chem. This killing and plundering brought on Ya'akov's curse, which scattered them among the tribes (Gen. 49:5–7, cf. Gen. 34).

Y'hudah's tribe absorbed Shim'on, and Levi received no land inheritance. Yet now Moshe blesses Levi as the nation's priests and Torah teachers, equipped with the tumim and urim (*perfections* and *lightings*) to hear from the LORD (Dt. 33:8, 10).

Munk [p. 384] observes that only Binyamin avoids Yisra'el's cardinal sins. He does not bow before Esav the idolater; nor does he join the plot to sell his brother Yosef (Gen. 33:1–3, Gen. 37).

Levi inherits the priesthood, but Binyamin inherits the Temple site.

When blessing Binyamin, Moshe calls him "y'did ADONAI" (*beloved of the LORD*, Dt. 33:12). Only this cherished son is born in the Land (Gen. 35:16–20), and the Ruach "hovers between his shoulders" (Dt. 33:12). Indeed, the Temple eventually is built in his land.

Read Dt. 33:9, cf. Mt. 10:32–36. Rashi comments that the L'vi'im put all idolaters, including their in-laws, to the sword at the apostasy of the golden calf. Relate safeguarding the covenant to your priestly relationship in Yeshua.

Blessing the Land

> ❝ *Of Yosef he said: "May* ADONAI *bless his land with the best from the sky, for the dew, and for what comes from the deep beneath . . ."* ❞
>
> —Deuteronomy 33:13

Blessings for Yosef from Moshe and Ya'akov display obvious parallels. In both cases, Yosef's tribe receives bountiful increases from heaven and earth.

Yosef receives blessings of abundance and power.

Historically speaking, Yosef blessed his brothers with abundance during a time of hardship. His actions saved the entire region from famine, while thrusting him to the top rank as the viceroy of Egypt. Now, Moshe blesses the tribe of Yosef with abundance of dew (the fruit of heaven) and abundance of "what the sun makes grow . . . with the best from the earth and all that fills it" (Dt. 33:13–16). Moshe adds power so Yosef, through Efrayim, may continue his role of treading upon the nations: majesty for his myriads, with horns to "gore the peoples, all of them, to the ends of the earth" (Dt. 33:17, cf. Gen. 49:26).

Thus, both Ya'akov and Moshe bless Yosef's younger son to continue his leadership role among the tribes (Gen. 48:14, 20; Dt. 33:17). Efrayim receives agricultural blessings in his lands and power over the nations of the world.

Read Dt. 33:17. Comment on Efrayim's title as "firstborn bull." Notice the blessing on "the head of Yosef, on the brow of the prince among his brothers" (Gen. 49:26). Explain why the exact same words are repeated in Dt. 33:16.

Blessing Torah Study

❝ *Of Z'vulun he said: "Rejoice, Z'vulun, as you go forth, and you, Yissakhar, in your tents."* **❞**

—Deuteronomy 33:18

Scripture itself refers to Ya'akov as an ish tam yoshev ohalim (*a wholesome man dwelling in tents,* Gen. 25:27). The sages credit Ya'akov with a proclivity to dwell in the house of study [Rashi, Gen.R. 63:10].

Moshe blesses the tribe of Yissakhar, saying, "Rejoice . . . in your tents" (Dt. 33:18). Rashi says that Leah's last two sons, Z'vulun and Yissakhar, form a holy partnership. Z'vulun prospers as a maritime merchant and funds the Torah study of Yissakhar. Z'vulun's name comes first, "because the Torah of Issachar can exist only because of Zebulun" [Munk, p. 387].

Moshe blesses both those who go out and those who dwell in tents.

The sages thrill over this partnership between the wealthy and the Torah scholar. R' Bachya says to pronounce Yissakhar as Yis-sachar, because each letter sin (*S*) has its own sachar (*reward*): the first for the one who studies Torah full-time and the second for the one who supports him [Munk, p. 387].

? *Noach, Avraham, and unblemished sacrifices are tamim (Gen. 6:9, 17:1, Lev. 1:3). Relate righteous sacrifice to Torah study (Gen. 25:27): "They will summon peoples to the mountain and there offer righteous sacrifices" (Dt. 33:19).*

Blessing the Water Supply

> ❝ *Of Dan he said: "Dan is a lion cub leaping forth from Bashan."* ❞
>
> —*Deuteronomy 33:22*

This segment includes blessings for all tribes that camped in the north and journeyed last as the rearguard (Num. 2:25–31). All three tribes are the sons of Ya'akov's concubines. Dan drinks from his streams in Bashan that unite at Leshem to become the Jordan River [Rashi]. Naftali "take[s] possession of the sea and the south" shores of the Galilee (Dt. 33:23). Asher will "bathe his feet in [olive] oil" in the fecund hills of upper Galilee [Dt. 33:24; Sifrei 355].

Tigay [pp. 521–522] observes that tribal listings follow a geographic order.

Standing in R'uven's territory, Moshe gazes over the river, north to Dan, south to Naftali, and west to Asher.

Blessed tribes and living waters fill the Land.

The segment includes one last verse that celebrates the coronation of the LORD as king over Yisra'el, affectionately idealized as Y'shurun (*Little Straight One*, Dt. 33:26). As Moshe finishes gazing, he seems to pan back and celebrate Yisra'el's good fortune under God's promised blessing to inherit a fertile Land.

Read Dt. 33:5, 26. Christensen [p. 837] sees Dt. 33:1–5 and Dt. 33:26–29 as two stanzas of an ancient hymn that surround Moshe's blessings of the twelve tribes (Dt. 33:6–25). Comment on the coronation of God as King over Y'shurun.

Groom of the Torah

❝ *The God of old is a dwelling-place,*
with everlasting arms beneath.
He expelled the enemy before you
and he said, "Destroy!" ❞   —Deuteronomy 33:27

Read on Simchat Torah, this section concludes portion, book, and Penteteuch. In Conservative congregations, wives accompany their husbands to read this segment, specially entitled the Chatan Torah (*bridegroom of the Torah*). Sephardic congregations call a newly married couple to read both from this segment and from the next segment. A second scroll is opened for this special reading, called the Chatan b'Reisheet (*bridegroom of Genesis/beginnings*).

Though not started until the ninth century, when the annual reading cycle became universally accepted, today's celebrations call every adult male to read from the Torah on Simchat Torah.

> *The end of Torah offers all*
> *a chance to ascend*
> *and read from the scroll.*

Next comes a special reading, observed even in Modern Orthodox congregations, called "Kol ha-Ne'arim (*All the Youngsters*)." Those under bar/bat mitzvah age chant the Torah blessings from the bimah (*platform*) and watch the Torah being read for them.

? *Actions speak louder than words. Thus, calling households and children to ascend the bimah to read Torah for themselves speaks mountains! How does the Chatan Torah segment relate to God and His covenant with Yisra'el?*

Groom of New Beginnings

❝ In the beginning God created the heavens and earth. ❞

—Genesis 1:1

New beginnings shatter old stereotypes. B'Reisheet's Haftarah (Is. 42:5–43:10, to be read next Shabbat) describes the day when the nations glorify God by silently affirming that only the God of Avraham has witnesses who have survived for thousands of years.

> ### New beginnings bring new solutions to old problems.

This century, survivors emerged from the camps of the Holocaust, and a nation was born in a day! Most assuredly, God has seen His people completely beaten down. Yet He has glorified Himself amidst His people and the nations (Dt. 32:36, 39, 43; Is. 42:17, 19; Is. 43:8–10).

At the present time, Yisra'el remains "partially blind" to Messiah, whereas the nations glory in the Good News that Yeshua has triumphed over death and ascended to the right hand of the Father. This same news makes Yisra'el red-faced, because God has yet to circumcise Yisra'el's heart (Dt. 30:6). Believers must enter God's promised rest (Heb. 4:2, 11) and fill Shabbat with its intended meaning.

? Read Hebrews 4:2, 9–11; explain how Yisra'el could hear the Good News, "but the message they heard didn't do them any good." God calls believers to "work hard and rest easy." How can you rest in Gan Eden as God intended?

Fulfilling All of the Torah

> " On the eighth day you are to have a festive
> assembly: you are not to do any kind of ordinary
> work; but you are to present a burnt offering . . . "
> —Numbers 29:35–36a

A question arises: why offer one bull for an olah (*ascent offering*)? This last of all convocation gatherings in the Torah is the least known and most mysterious of all holy convocations.

Sh'mini Atseret is for those who most love God.

At Sukkot, the priesthood offers seventy bulls for the seventy nations of the world, as God judges the world regarding rainfall on Sukkot [R.H. 16a; cf. Zech. 14:16–17]. Thus, the nations are assured rain, because the priesthood offers atonement for the world at Sukkot. Sh'mini Atseret (*Eighth* day of *Restraint*), a separate festival in its own right, follows Sukkot's seventh day.

Now, the sages answer this most mysterious question about a single bull on Sh'mini Atseret: "It corresponds to the singular nation of Israel. This can be compared to a king . . . who said . . . the final day of the banquet . . . to his beloved companion: 'Prepare for me a small meal so that I may enjoy your company'" [Sukk. 55b].

? When the nations go home, the king turns to tell his inner court, "Tarry with me an extra day." Recalling that the watchmen on the walls of Y'rushalayim cry, "Blessed is he who comes in the name of the LORD," explain Mt. 23:37–39.

Y'hoshua Succeeds Moshe

Meander

> **"** *After the death of Moshe the servant of ADONAI, ADONAI said to Y'hoshua the son of Nun, Moshe's assistant, "Moshe my servant is dead. So now, get up and cross over this Yarden . . .* **"** — Joshua 1:1–2

Following Moshe's death, God raises up Y'hoshua by commanding him to cross over the Yarden to take the Land (Josh. 1:1–2).

Tigay [p. 417] asserts that this Haftarah is intended to parallel the Chatan B'REISHEET (Gen. 1:1–2:3). In a custom still observed today, Babylonian and Kurdish Jews read sections from the Torah, Prophets, and Writings—all at the same time.

Continuities in leadership also go hand and glove with the "chain of tradition" from Moshe to the Prophets [M. Avot 1], which expands Torah to Tanakh (*Torah, Prophets, and Writings*).

Y'hoshua succeeds Moshe.

Connections between God's orders, Moshe's words, and Y'hoshua's mandate link the books of Deuteronomy and Joshua. God commands Y'hoshua to take the Land He has promised (Josh. 1:3, cf. Dt. 11:24). He further exhorts Y'hoshua with the powerful imperative, "Be strong! Be bold!" (Josh. 1:6, 9; cf. Dt. 31:7–8).

> **?** *Talmud explains that this week's original Haftarah related Moshe's blessing on the tribes (Dt. 33) with Sh'lomo's blessing at the Temple [1 Ki. 8:22ff., see Meg. 31b]. What emerged as the more central message of this new Haftarah?*

> ❝ *Night will no longer exist, so they will need neither the light of a lamp nor the light of the sun, because ADONAI, God, will shine upon them. And they will reign as kings forever and ever.* ❞ —Rev. 22:5

The message of Torah expands to Tanakh and its renewal in the B'rit Chadashah. Y'hoshua continues Moshe's journey to inherit the Promised Land.

Yeshua and the B'rit Chadashah further expand upon the promises of God.

In this passage, the faithful behold "the holy city, Y'rushalayim, coming down out of heaven from God" (Rev. 21:9–10). Moshe's forty-day experience B'HAR (*on the Mount*) becomes the holy city's thousand-year reign as one unending, glory-filled, Shabbat.

With Satan bound, the curse and the night end (Rev. 21:25; 22:3, 5). The city's inhabitants require neither lamp by night nor sun by day, because ADONAI "will shine upon them. And [His servants] will reign as kings forever" (Rev. 22:5).

Most incredibly, "the throne of God and of the Lamb will be in the city, and his servants will worship him; they will see his face, and his name will be on their foreheads" (Rev. 22:4). Thus, those in Y'rushalayim live in glorious, luminous, pure proximity to the Presence of our holy God.

❓ *Read Rev. 21:27. Comment on why "nothing impure" may enter Y'rushalayim. Read Rev. 21:1–2, cf. 21:9–10.*
● *Are Y'rushalayim and New Y'rushalayim the same city? Note Rev. 21:25, cf. Gen. 3:22–24. Why do the gates stay open?*

Talk Your Walk . . .

Always read on Simchat Torah, Parashat V'ZOT HAB'RACHAH (*and this the blessing*) concludes the annual reading cycle of Torah and begins it anew. The name of the portion signals that God's blessings outweigh the curses. Accordingly, Moshe blesses the tribal land inheritances, Torah study, and living waters in the Land. The last section, the Chatan TORAH (*bridegroom of the Torah*) links with the first segment, the Chatan B'REISHEET (*bridegroom of Genesis*). Then the maftir (*concluding*) section skips to a seven-verse reading about the concluding convocation day of Torah, Sh'mini Atseret (*the eighth* day of *restraint*), when God's elect enjoy special time in His Presence.

The Haftarah, read from the first verses of N'vi'im (*the Prophets*), connects back to Torah by linking the leadership succession of Y'hoshua with the passing of Moshe. Looking forward, this reading parallels the reading from the portion B'REISHEET by connecting new beginnings with the next generation's entering the Land to claim its God-given inheritance.

> **God calls mankind to dwell in His Presence.**

The B'rit Chadashah builds upon the expansion of God's Word (from Torah to Prophets to Renewed Covenant) and also upon Yisra'el's call to dwell in the place God chooses to put His name. For Yisra'el, that place is Y'rushalayim. For Moshe and those who draw near, it is that day when God's elect see Him "face to face."

Oasis

. . . Walk Your Talk

D o you secretly harbor Moshe's heartfelt desire to see God in His glory? Do you dismiss the thought as a wish that can never be? Is this wise? Perhaps you have told yourself, "I can never be as pure of heart as Moshe, who talked to God and asked to see His glory, but was denied."

Yet Messiah tells us plainly, "How blessed are the pure in heart, for they will see God" (Mt. 5:8). Do not think for a moment that God will refuse to circumcise your heart, if you ask Him and show willingness to go the distance. It's not home-grown purity you must manufacture, but rather a *willingness* to seek God and to ante up when God calls you to obey.

God calls you to mature in your faith. Every day brings new decisions. You can choose to increase your own self or Messiah's budding image within you: "So all of us, with faces unveiled, see as in a mirror the glory of the LORD; and we are being changed into his very image, from one degree of glory to the next, by ADONAI the Spirit" (2 Cor. 3:18). Are you willing to let the

> *Transformation is going full circle and knowing the start for the first time.*

Ruach complete building the New Man within you? Will you walk the journey to its resting place?

Shabbat Shalom!

efer D'VARIM concludes when its final portion is read on Simchat Torah. Moshe spends the entire book preparing Yisra'el to enter the inheritance God promised the Fathers long ago. But inheriting is no easy task. Moshe himself is shut out in his lifetime. He sternly warns Yisra'el to safeguard the covenant.

The final portion, V'ZOT HAB'RACHAH (*and this the blessing*) concludes with a return to Gan Eden (Chatan B'REISHEET reading) on Sh'mini Atseret (Maftir reading). The nations of the earth rejoice and sing God's praises with Yisra'el (Dt. 32:43). At the conclusion of Sukkot, as the nations are returning home, the LORD turns to his innermost court and says: Atsor (*tarry*) in Y'rushalayim for one more day!

Does this exclusive invitation kindle jealousy in you? Isaiah prophesies that the Gentiles will come to Y'rushalayim, bringing the sons of Yisra'el as a minchah (*grain offering*). V'gam-meihem (*also from among them*, i.e. the Gentiles), God says, ekach la-kohanim la-l'vi'im (*I will take for priests, for Levites*, Is. 66:21). Amazed, Rashi

> **Jews and Gentiles celebrate God's glory!**

connects this sod (*mystery*) to Dt. 29:29(28 הַדָּבָר), "stated long before" [Fishbane, pp. 327, 331]. Rav Sha'ul connects this same mystery to God's calling of foreigners as New Covenant kohanim (Ro. 11:25–27).

Perhaps God has intended from the very beginning that _all_ humanity would draw near to worship Him forever! God will build His priesthood from the living stones of all nations (1 Pet. 2:4–5). Search yourself! Only those with circumcised hearts will tarry.

End

What can be more glorious than maturing into an offering wholly dedicated to the LORD? Yet if Yisra'el is the offering, the Gentiles who present this offering are numbered among the kohanim and Levites. Distinctions between Jews and Gentiles, men and women, rich and poor, pass away as we all behold God's glory together.

For now, divisions remain. Gentile believers look upon God's glory in the heavenlies with eyes veiled by faith. Yet they do not fully comprehend the magnitude of their priestly privileges. Meanwhile, corporate Yisra'el, though chosen, remains veiled and hostile to the Good News of Messiah's death and resurrection.

God showed kindness to King David, the anointed forebearer of Messiah (Ro. 15:9, cf. 2 Sam. 22:50). Through the Son of David, God establishes His throne in chesed ve'emet. Indeed, with this *covenant kindness and truth*, Yeshua will rule all nations for a thousand years and forevermore (Ro. 15:10, cf. Dt. 32:43).

Cleave to God as He

> **God establishes His throne in kindness and truth.**

establishes His covenant. Rule with Him as His kind, but passionate priesthood. God's kindness will turn aside His curse. As His priests, we can beseech God to grant kindness and blessing to Yisra'el and all who would glorify His name. Be strong, be strong, and may we be strengthened to finish the journey!

Chazak, Chazak, v'Nit'chazek!

We hear Moshe's d'rash
on Moab's plains.
The manna will stop,
we'll feast on the grains.
We roll the Torah
back to the start . . .
to fresh beginnings,
renewed in heart.
So enter the Promise
for Messiah's sake.
Chazak, Chazak, v'Nit'chazek!

חֲזַק חֲזַק וְנִתְחַזֵּק
*Be strong, be strong,
and may we be strengthened!!!*

Glossary

ACHAREI MOT (*after the death*)

adamah (*land*)

ADONAI (*the LORD/*יהוה)

ADONAI ha-holech lifneichem (*the LORD is the One Who walks before you*)

ADONAI he'emir'cha ha-yom lih'yot lo l'am s'gullah ka'asher diber-lach (*ADONAI has declared you today to be to Him a most-treasured people, just as He promised you*)

ADONAI hu ha-holech l'fane-icha (*the LORD, He is the One Who walks before you*)

Aharon (*Aaron*)

airei (*Greek for* cuts off)

aliyah (*go up*)

al sefer ad tumam (*upon a document, until complete*)

al-tosef daber elai od ba-davar ha-zeh (*do not continue to speak to Me anymore about this matter*)

'Amalek (*Amalek*)

am-chacham v'navon (*a people, wise and understanding*)

Amidah (*standing prayer*)

am-kadosh (*a holy people*)

am-k'sheh-oref (*a stiff-necked people*)

am naval (*foolish people*)

'Amorah (*Gomorrah*)

am s'gulah (*treasured people*)

ana ADONAI, hoshi'a na (*please now, O LORD, save now!*)

ani ADONAI b'itahh achishenah (*I am the LORD, in its time I will quicken it*)

Anochi, Anochi hu m'nachemchem (*I, I am He who comforts you*)

anochi haster astir panai (*I, I will conceal, yes conceal my face*, Fox transl., Dt. 31:18)

arami oved avi (*an Aramean, the wandering/ perishing one, my father*)

arur asher lo-yakim et-divrei
ha-torah-ha-zot la'asot otam
(*a curse on the one who does
not establish the words of this
Torah, to do them*)

asher anochi me'id bachem
ha-yom (*which I testify
against you this day*)

asher t'tsavum et-b'neichem
(*which you are to command
your children*)

Ashkenazim, Ash. (middle and
northern European Jews)

astirah fanai meihem ereh
mah acharitam (*I will hide My
face from them, I will see what
will be their later experience*)

atah tan'chilenah otam (*you
will be the one causing them to
inherit it*)

atem nitsavim (*you are [still]
standing*)

atem nitsavim ha-yom (*you all
are standing this day*)

atsarot (*assemblies*)

atseret (*restraint*)

atsor (*tarry*)

Avot (*Fathers*/also name of
first part of Amidah prayer)

Avraham (*Abraham*)

Avram (*Abram*)

ayin (16th letter of the Hebrew
alefbet)

BALAK (*Balak/destroyer*)

bar/bat mitzvah (*son/daughter*

of the commandment; religious
rite of passage to adulthood)

baruch haba b'shem ADONAI
(*blessed is he who comes in the
name of the LORD*)

baruch tih'yeh mi-kol-ha-
amim (*blessed shall you be
from all of the peoples*)

BCE (Before the Common Era)

b'chol-l'vav'cha oo-v'chol-nafshecha (*with all your heart
and with all your soul*)

B'CHUKOTAI (*in My statutes*)

be'er et-ha-torah ha-zot (*an
expounding on this Torah*)

Beit-Anyah (*Bethany, house of
poverty*)

Beit-P'or (*Beth-peor*)

Betser (*Bezer*)

b'ever haYarden (*across/on
the far side of the Jordan*)

b'ever haYarden ba-midbar
ba-Aravah mol Suf bein-
Paran oo-vein-Tofel v'Lavan
va-Chatserot v'Di Zahav
(*across the Jordan, in the wilderness on the plain opposite Suph,
between Paran and Tophel,
Laban, Hazeroth, and Di-Zahab*)

b'ever haYarden miz'r'chah
shamesh (*across the Jordan,
toward the rising of the sun*)

b'ficha (*in your mouth*)

B'HA'ALOT'CHA (*in your making
go up*)

B'HAR (*on the Mount*)

biarta ha-**ra'** mi-kir**be**cha (*you will burn out the evil from your midst*)

big**dei-ye**sha (*in garments of salvation*)

bi**mah** (*platform*)

Binyamin (*Benjamin*)

B'MIDBAR (*in the wilderness or in the wilderness of*)

B'MIDBAR Sinai (*in the wilderness of Sinai*)

b'mo'**ed** sh'**nat** ha-sh'**mittah** b'**chag** ha-suk**kot** (*at the appointed-time of the Year of Release, on the pilgrimage-festival of Sukkot*)

b'**nei** Yisra'**el** (*children of Israel*)

BO (*enter!*)

b'oz**nei** ha'**am** (*in the ears of the people*)

b'oz**nei** kol-k'**hal** Yisra'**el** et-div**rei** ha-shi**rah** ha-**zot** ad tu**mam** (*in the ears of the whole assembly of Israel, the words of this song to their completion*)

B'REISHEET (*in the beginning*)

B'rit Chada**shah** (*New Covenant/New Testament*)

b'**rit** olam (*everlasting covenant*)

B'SHALACH (*when he let go*)

b'**shem** ADONAI (*in the name of the LORD*)

b'tsid'**kati** (*in my righteous-merit*)

B'ulah (*Espoused*)

chalut**sim** (lit. *pioneer, "shock troops"*)

cha**mas** (*lawlessness, violence*)

chami**shi** (*fifth*)

cha**tan** (*bridegroom*)

Chatse**rot** (*Hazeroth*)

chatta'**t** (*sin/purification offering*)

CHAYEI SARAH (*the life of Sarah*)

cha**zak**, cha**zak**, v'nit'cha**zek** (*be strong, be strong, and may we be strengthened*)

Chazal (לז״ח, an acronym for Chachamei**nu** Zichro**nam** Li-v'ra**chah**/*our sages of blessed memory*)

Cheftsi-**vahh** (*I delight in her*)

che**lek** k'che**lek** (*portion by portion*)

che**sed** (*covenant kindness*)

che**sed** ve'**emet** (*covenant kindness and truth*)

Chev**ron** (*Hebron*)

chiz**ku** v'imt**su** (*be strong and courageous*)

Chorev (*Horeb*)

CHUKAT (*statute of*)

chu**kim** (*statutes*)

C'**na'**an (*Canaan*)

C'na'**ani** (*Canaanite*)

C'na'**anim** (*Canaanites*)

cohen/cohanim—see kohen

dalet (4th letter of the Hebrew alefbet)

dam-e**nav** tishteh-**cha**mer (*blood of grapes, you drank fermented*)

da**rga**-t'**vir** (*broken step, two trope marks indicating patterns for cantillation*)

da**var** (*word/case/matter/legal matter/thing*; pl. d'varim)

dor l'**dor** (*generation to generation*)

d'**rash** (*inquiry, homily*)

D'var-Adonai (*the Word of the Lord*)

D'varim (*words*)

'ed (עד, *witness*)

Ef**ra**yim (*Ephraim*)

Ei**chah** (*How?...*)

ei**ne**nu shome**a** b'**ko**lenu (*he does not listen to our voice*)

Ei**val** (*Ebal*)

e**kach** la-koha**nim** la-l'vi'**im** (*I will take for priests, for Levites*)

Ekev (*as a result, as a result of*)

ekev asher shamata b'koli (*as a result that you listened to My Voice*)

ekev tish'**m'un et** ha-mishpa-**tim** (*as a result of your hearkening to the regulations*)

e**lav** tishma'**un** (*to him shall you listen*)

eleh ha-d'va**rim** (*these are the words*)

Eli**faz** (*Eliphaz*)

Eli**ya**hu (*Elijah*)

Emor (*say!*)

er**vat** da**var** (*something of 'nakedness'*)

E**sav** (*Esau*)

et-Adonai he'emar**ta** lih'**yot** l'**cha** le**lo**him ... v'la**le**chet ... v'lish**mor** ... v'lishmo'a b'ko-**lo** (*the Lord you have declared to be to you God ... to walk ... to observe ... and to listen to His Voice*)

et-ha-**b'rit** v'et-ha-**che**sed (*keep ... the covenant and covenant kindness*)

et-**kol** divrei-**chem** (*the voice of your words*)

Gadi (*Gadite*)

Gan Eden (*the Garden of Eden/Paradise*)

ger (*alien, resident sojourner, stranger*)

ge**rim** (*resident aliens*)

geshem (*rain*)

Gil'ad (*Gilead*)

go'el (*redeemer*)

go**yim** (*gentiles, nations*)

G'rizim (*Gerizim*)

Ha'azinu (*give ear!*)

haChitti (*Hittites*)

haC'na'ani (*Canaanites*)

ha-d'varim (*the words*)

ha-d'vei**kim** ba'Adonai (*those who cleave to the Lord*)

ha-El, ha-Gadol, ha-Gibor, v'ha-Nora (*the great, mighty,*

and awesome God)

ha-**El** ha-ne'**eman** sho**mer** ha-**b'rit** v'ha-**chesed** (*the faithful God, who safeguards the covenant and covenant kindness*)

haEmo**ri** (*Amorites*)

Haft**arah** (*conclusion*/reading from Prophets; pl. Hafta**rot**)

hagba**hah** (lit. *elevating*, a ritual in which the Torah scroll is raised for all to see after a public reading)

ha-ho**lech** lifnei**chem** (*the One Who walks before you*)

hak'**hel** (*assembly*, gathering of people to listen as king reads Torah every seven years; Dt. 31:10–13)

hak'**hilu** e**lai** et-kol-zik**nei** shivtei**chem** v'shotrei**chem** (*assemble to me all of your elders and tribal officials*)

Hala**chah**/Hala**khah** (*Hebrew Law*)

haL'vi'**im** (*the Levites*)

haMa**kom** Go**rem** (lit. *the place influences the event*)

Har G'ri**zim** (*Mt. Gerizim*)

Har N'**vo** (*Mt. Nebo*)

haY'**vusi** (*Jebusites, Yevusites*)

Hem kin'**uni** v'lo-**el**/kia**suni** b'havlei**hem**//v'**ani** akni**em** b'lo-**am**/b'**goi** na**val** achi**sem** (*They made Me red-faced with*

a No-god/angered Me with their transitoriness//so I will make them red-faced with a no-people/with a nation of fools I will anger them*)

hish'mi'**acha** et-ko**lo** l'yas'**srecha** (*He caused you to hear His Voice in order to discipline you*)

Hosha**na** Rab**bah** (*the great hosanna, 7th day of Sukkot*)

hoshi'a **na** (*save now, please!*)

hu ha-ho**lech** i**mach** (*He is the One Who walks with you*)

hu ha-nil**cham** la-**chem** (*He is the One Who wages war for you*)

ish tam yo**shev** oha**lim** (*a wholesome man dwelling in tents*)

jihad (*holy war initiated by the Voice of God*)

ka'**asher** ta'**asei**nah ha-d'vo**rim** (*just as bees do*)

ka'**asher** za**mam** la'**asot** l'a**chiv** (*just as he schemed to do to his brother*)

ka**desh** (*sanctification*)

Kalev (*Caleb*)

kash**rut** (*kosher laws*)

ka**thai**rei (*Greek for* trims)

Kayin (*Cain*)

K'DOSHIM (*holy ones*)

Kefa (*Peter*)

K'**hat** (*Kohath*)

ki am kadosh atah l'Adonai Eloheicha (*because you are a holy people for the* Lord *your God*)

ki chashalta ba'avonecha (*for you have stumbled in your iniquity*)

ki im-shamor tish'm'run et-kol-ha-mitzvah ha-zot (*for if, keeping, you will keep all this commandment*)

ki-karov eleicha ha-davar m'od (*the word is very close to you*)

ki lo-davar rek hu mi-kem (*not an empty word is it for you*)

Ki Tavo (*when you enter in*)

Ki Tetse (*when you go out*)

Ki Tisa (*when you elevate*)

Kivrot ha-Ta'avah (*Kibroth Hattaavah/graves of the craving*)

kluv (*basket*)

k'naf'sh'cha sav'echa (*according to your soul your fullness,* i.e. to satisfy your appetite)

kodesh kodashim (*Holy of Holies; especially holy offerings*)

kohen/kohanim (*priest/priests*)

Kohen Gadol (*High Priest*)

kol adat Yisra'el (*the whole community of Israel*)

kol-b'nei-chayil (*all sons of cal-iber,* or "*shock-troops*")

kol-ha-mitsvah, v'ha-chukim v'ha-mishpatim, asher t'lamdem (*the whole commandment, both the statutes and the regulations, that you are to teach them*)

kol ha-ne'arim (*all the youngsters*)

Kol-Nidrei (evening service of Yom Kippur, lit. *all vows of*)

Korach (*Korah/bald*)

Korinaiazo (Greek, *to act like a Corinthian,* i.e. to commit fornication)

kosher (*fit;* also kasher)

la'asotam (*to do them*)

l'ahavah et-Adonai eloheicha lish'mo'a b'kolo ul'davkah-vo (*to love the* Lord *your God, to listen to His Voice, and to cleave to Him*)

l'ahavah v'la'avod (*to love and to serve*)

lalechet (*to walk*)

latset v'lavo (*to go out and to come in*)

lavaz (*plunder*)

l'davkah-vo (*to cleave to Him*)

Lech L'Cha (*go forth, yourself!*)

l'hach'iso (*vexing Him*)

l'ir'ah (*to hold-in-awe*)

lishmor (*to safeguard*)

lo-emun bam (*there is no faith in them*)

lo-kidasht**em** o**ti** (*you did not sanctify Me*)

lo nucha**m**ah (*uncomforted*)

l'ov'**r'cha** bi-v'**rit** . . . u'v'alat**o** (*to cross over into covenant . . . and into its oath-of-fealty*)

lo tira'**um** (*you shall not fear them*)

lo v'tsidka**t'cha** (*not in your righteousness*)

lo-yit'yat**sev ish** bifnei-**chem** (*no man will take-a-stand in your face*)

l'so**nav** el-pa**nav** (*to the one who hates Him to his face*)

L'vi'**im** (*Levites*)

LXX (Septuagint, Greek trans. of Heb. Scriptures)

ma'a**ser** (*tithe, tenth*)

ma'a**ser** she**ni** (*second tithe*)

maf**tir** (*concluding*)

malt**em** or**lat** l'vav'**chem** (*you must peel away/circumcise the thickening of your heart*)

mam**le**chet koha**nim** v'**goy** ka**dosh** (*kingdom of priests and a holy nation*)

mam**zer** (*product of a forbidden marriage*)

Mas'**ei** (*journeys of*)

Mas'**ei** b'nei Yisra'**el** (*the journeys of the sons of Yisra'el*)

Mas**sah** (*testing*)

Ma**tot** (*tribes*)

mat**zah** (*unleavened bread*)

me'**ever** l'Yar**den** (*from across the Jordan*)

Mekhil**ta** (Aramaic, lit. *measure* or *method*, Tannaitic Midrash on Exodus)

melech (*king*)

me-**rosh** par'**ot** o**yev** (*from the head of the leaders of the enemy*)

mi**dot** k'**neg**ed mi**dot** (*measure for measure*)

Mid**rash** (*inquiry, rabbinical commentary on the Bible*)

mid**rash** (*study, sermon, homiletic interpretation*)

mi**Ketz** (*at the end of*)

mi**ketz** she**va** sha**nim** (*at the end of seven years*)

mi**kra** bikku**rim** (*recitation of firstfruits*)

mikra-**ko**desh (*holy convocation*)

min**chah** (*grain offering, tribute, meal offering*)

min**chat** bikku**rim** (tribute of first-processed)

min-ha-mid**bar** v'ha-l'va**non** (*from the wilderness to Lebanon*)

min-ha-na**har** N'har-P'**rat** v'**ad** ha-**yam** ha-acha**ron** (*from the river, River Euphrates, to the last sea, i.e. Mediterranean*)

min**yan** (lit. *number/quorum of 10 adults for public prayer*) mishkan (*tabernacle/dwelling/ God's dwelling*)

Mishnah (*teachings, the Oral Law compiled in 220 CE*)

mishpat (*justice*)

MISHPATIM (*judgments, ordinances, regulations*)

mitsvot (*commands*)

Mitzrayim (*Egypt*)

M'nasheh (*Manasseh*)

Mo'av (*Moab*)

Moshe (*Moses*)

M'rivat-Kadesh (*Meribah of Kadesh, "Striving of Holiness"*)

m'shalem . . . l'ha'avido (*the One Who repays . . . by causing him to perish*)

M'TSORA (*infected one*)

Musaf (an *additional* service)

Nachamu, nachamu ami (*comfort, comfort My people*)

Naftali (*Naphtali*)

nakam (*vengeance without revenge, defensive vindication*)

NASO (*elevate!*)

navi (*prophet*)

nefesh (*soul*)

NITSAVIM (*standing*)

NOACH (*Noah/rest*)

nochri (*foreigner*)

Numeruwechsel (German, lit. *number change*, a change from plural to singular or vice versa, indicating a change in structure)

n'veilah (*the carcass of an animal that died of itself*)

n'vi'im (*prophets*)

'Og (*Og*)

Ohel Mo'ed (*Tent of Meeting*)

olah (*ascent offering; burnt or whole offering*)

olat tamid (*daily/regular ascent offering*)

olot (*ascent offerings*)

ot (*sign*)

ovrim (*they cross over*, same root as Ivrim/*Hebrews*)

panim b'fanim (*face in face*)

parashah (Torah *portion*)

parashat (*portion of*)

parashiot (Torah *portions*, pl.)

Par'oh (*Great House, Pharaoh*)

Pesach (*Passover*)

PINCHAS (*Phinehas/dark-skinned*)

P'KUDEI (*accountings of*)

P'rushim (*Pharisees*)

p'sol-l'cha (*carve for yourself*)

Radak (Rabbi David Kimchi)

Rambam (Rabbi Moshe ben Maimon, Maimonides)

Ramban (Rabbi Moshe ben Nachman, Nachmanides)

Rashi (Rabbi Shlomo ben Itzchak)

Rav (*Rabbi/Great One*)

rav-lach (*enough for you!*)

rav-lachem (*enough for you!, too much for you!*)

rav l'hoshia (*mighty to save*)
Rav Sha'ul (*Paul*)
R'EH (*see!*)
R'eh! . . . Aleh! Resh! (*See! . . . Go up! Take possession!*)
Re'uveni (CJB), R'uveni (*Reubenites*)
R'fidim (*Rephidim*)
rishon (*first*)
rishonim (*first generation*)
riv (*lawsuit*)
Rosh haShanah (*the Head of the Year*)
ruach (*wind, spirit*)
Ruach haKodesh (*Holy Spirit*)
R'uven (*Reuben*)
r'vi'i (*fourth*)
sachar (*reward*)
S'dom (*Sodom*)
Sefer B'MIDBAR (*Book of Numbers/in the wilderness*)
Sefer B'REISHEET (*Book of Genesis/in the beginning*)
Sefer D'VARIM (*Book of Deuteronomy/words*)
Sefer HAD'VARIM (*the Book of Words*)
sefer ha-torah ha-zeh (*the document of this Torah*)
Sefer SH'MOT (*Book of Exodus/names*)
Sefer VAYIKRA (*Book of Leviticus/then He called*)
Se'ir (*Seir*)
Sephardic (pertaining to Sephardim, Jews of Spanish descent; abbrev. Seph.)
Sephardim (Jews of Spanish descent, also N. Africa and Middle East; abbrev. Seph.)
S'fardim, see Sephardim
Shabbat (*Sabbath*)
Shabbat Nachamu (*the Sabbath of Consolation*)
Shabbat Shuvah (*the Sabbath of Return*)
Shabbat T'shuvah (*the Sabbath of Repentance*)
shamanta avita casita (*you grew fat, thick, gross!*)
shamarta et-ha-mitsvah, v'et-ha-chukim v'et-ha-mishpa-tim (*you shall keep the commandment, the laws and the rulings*)
shamor (*safeguard*)
Sha'ul (*Saul/Paul*)
shav . . . et-sh'vut'cha (lit. *He returns your return*, idiom for *He restores your fortunes*)
Shavu'ot (lit. *weeks*, Feast of Weeks, Pentecost)
sheni (*second*)
sheva minim (*seven species*, i.e. grapes, olives, dates, figs, pomegranates, wheat, and barley)
Shirat David (*song of David*)
Shirat Moshe (*song of Moses*)
shishi (*sixth*)

Sh'LACH L'CHA (*send for your-self!*)

sh'lamim (*fellowship offerings*)

shlishi (*third*)

Sh'lomo (*Solomon*)

Sh'ma, Yisra'el! ADONAI Eloheinu, ADONAI echad (*Hear, Isra'el! ADONAI our God, ADONAI is one*)

Sh'ma Yisra'el and v'ahavta (*Hear O Israel . . . and you shall love . . .*)

SH'MINI (*eighth*)

Sh'mini Atseret (*the eighth* day of *restraint*, last convocation day of the Torah, celebrated at the end of Sukkot)

sh'mittah (*release*)

SH'MOT (*names/Exodus*)

SHOF'TIM (*judges*)

shof'tim v'shot'rim (*judges and officials*)

shoresh poreh rosh v'la'anah (*a root-bearing fruit of worm-wood and poison-herb*)

Shuvah Yisra'el (*Return Yisra'el*)!

shvi'i (*seventh*)

Sichon (*Sihon*)

simach et-ishto (*he shall glad-den his wife*)

Simchat Beit haSho'evah (*the joy of the water drawing*)

Simchat Torah (*joy of the Torah*)

sin'at chinam (*baseless hatred*)

som tasim aleicha melech (*you may set, yes set, over you a king*)

sos asis ba'ADONAI (*I will rejoice intensely in the* LORD)

S'udat haAdon (*the Lord's Supper*)

Sukkot (*Succoth, huts, booths*)

ta'aseh ha-yashar (*you will do the right thing*)

ta'avodu (*serve*)

tahor (*ritually clean*)

talmidim (*students/disciples*)

Talmud (*commentary on the Mishnah*)

tamei (*ritually impure/conta-gious/defiled*)

tamim (*perfect*)

tamim tih'yeh (*wholehearted shall you be*)

Tammuz (fourth month in the Hebrew calendar)

Tanakh (תנ״ך, an acronym for the Hebrew canon; *Torah*, *N'vi'im/Prophets*, and *K'tuvim/Writings*)

tapp'chem (*your little ones, tod-dlers*)

Tav'erah (*Taberah*, lit. *blazing*)

TAZRIA (*she bears seed*)

telechu (*you shall walk*)

Tetragrammaton, יהוה (*Yod-Hay-Vav-Hay; the four-letter name of* ADONAI)

t'fillin (*phylacteries, prayer*

boxes)

T'hillah (*Praise*)

tid'bakun (*you shall cleave*)

tira'u (*hold-in-awe*)

Tish'ah b'Av (*ninth of Av*, fast day commemorating the destruction of both Temples)

tish'moru (*obey*)

TOL'DOT (*generations, life story, offspring*)

Torah (*instruction*/Penteteuch, Genesis-Deuteronomy)

trope (mark used for cantillation, also called ta'am/*flavor*)

T'RUMAH (*offering*)

tsadikim (*righteous ones*)

tsadik v'yashar hu (*righteous and straight is He*)

TSAV (*command!*)

ts'dakah (*righteous merit*)

t'shuvah (*return*)

Tsiyon (*Zion*)

tsur (*Rock*)

T'TSAVEH (*you shall command*)

tumim and urim (*perfections and lightings*)

Tziyon (*Zion*)

u'v'kolo tishma'u (*and to His Voice hearken*)

va'azavani v'hefer et-b'riti (*they will abandon Me and break My covenant*)

VAERA (*and I appeared*)

VA'ET'CHANAN (*and I pleaded*)

v'atah tashuv v'shamata b'kol

ADONAI v'asita et-kol-mitsvotav (*you will return, listen to God's Voice, and do all His commands*)

VAYAKHEL (*and he assembled*)

VAY'CHI (*and he lived*)

VAYELECH (*and went*)

va-yelech Moshe (*Moshe went out*)

VAYERA (*and He appeared*)

VAYESHEV (*and he settled*)

VAYETSE (*and he went out*)

VAYIGASH (*and he drew near*)

VAYIKRA (*and He called/ Leviticus*)

VAYISHLACH (*and he sent*)

va-yish'ma ADONAI et-kol divreichem (*and the LORD listened to the voice of your words*)

v'chol-banayich limudei ADONAI, v'rav sh'lom banayich (*all your children will be taught of the LORD, and great shall be the well-being of your children*)

v'et asher einenu poh (*with the one who is not here*)

v'gam-meihem (*also from among them*)

v'hayah ki-yavo'u aleicha kol-ha-d'varim ha-eleh, ha-b'rachah v'ha-k'lalah (*now it will be that when all these words/matters come upon you, the blessing and the curse*)

v'**lo** tach**ati** et-ha-**aretz** (*do not bring sin upon the Land*)

v'**ram** l'vav**echa**, v'shachach**ta** et-ADONAI (*proud-hearted, you forget the* LORD)

v'**sham**ah **lo tavo** (*but to there, you shall not enter*)

v'**shamanu** v'**asinu** (*we will hearken and we will do*)

v'**shamata** b'**kol** ADONAI (*you must listen to the Voice of the* LORD)

v'**ZOT HAB'RACHAH** (*and this the blessing*)

v'**zot** haTo**rah** asher-**sam** Mo**she** lif**nei** b'**nei** Yisra'**el** (*this is the Torah which Moses placed before the children of Israel*)

Ya'a**kov** (*Jacob*)

Ya**bok** (*Jabbok*)

Yam-**Suf** (*Sea of Reeds*)

Yar**den** (*Jordan*)

Yarov'**am** (*Jeroboam*)

ya**shuv** ADONAI la**sus** ale**icha** l'**tov** (*The* LORD *will return to rejoice over you for good*)

Y'chez**kel** (*Ezekiel*)

Ye**hu** (*Jehu*)

Yesha'**yahu** (*Isaiah*)

Ye**shu**a (*Jesus/salvation*)

Ye**shu**a haMashi**ach** (*Jesus the Messiah*)

Y'ho**shu**a (*Joshua, lit. God is*

salvation)

Y'hu**dah** (*Judah*)

Y'hu**dah** haNasi (*Judah, the Leader*, compiler of Mishnah)

Yirm'**yahu** (*Jeremiah*)

Yisra'**el** (*Israel*)

Yisra'**elim** (*Israelis, Israelites*)

Yissa**khar** (*Issachar*)

YI**TRO** (*Jethro/abundance*)

Yitz**chak** (*Isaac*)

Yom-Kip**pur** (*Day of Atonement*)

Yo**sef** (*Joseph*)

Y'**recho** (*Jericho*)

y'**rushah** (*possession*)

Y'rushalayim (*Jerusalem*)

Y'**shu'ah** (*Salvation*)

Y'shu**run** (*Jeshurun, Little Straight One*)

Y'**vusi** (*Jebusite/Yebusite*)

za**chor** (*remember*)

Zamzum**mim** (*Zamzummim*)

Z'char**yah** (*Zechariah*)

ze**vach** sh'la**mim** (*sacrifice of well-being;* often called a *peace offering*)

z'man simcha**teinu** (*the time of our rejoicing*)

Z'vu**lun** (*Zebulun*)

יהוה (See *Tetragrammaton*.)

תנ״ך (If verse numbers vary, Hebrew references show this symbol. See *Tanakh*.)

Bibliography

Abarbanel, Isaac ben Judah, also Abravanel. See Stone Edition, Scherman, Rabbi Nosson (Gen. Ed.).

Abravanel, see Abarbanel.

Alcalay, Reuben. *The Complete English-Hebrew, Hebrew-English Dictionary.* Ramat Gan: Massadah Publishing Co., 1981.

Arach., Arachin, see Schorr, *Talmud Bavli.*

Archer, Gleason L. and Chirchigno, G.C. *Old Testament Quotations in the New Testament: A Complete Survey.* Chicago: Moody Press, 1983.

Attridge, Harold W. *The Epistle to the Hebrews.* In Helmut Koester (Gen. Ed.), *Hermeneia.* Philadelphia: Fortress Press, 1989.

Avot, Pirkei Avot, see *The Metsudah Pirkei Avos: The Wisdom of the Fathers.*

Av. Zar., Avodah Zarah, see Schorr, *Talmud Bavli.*

Baraita, D'melechet haMishkan, 13, cited in Ramban

Barrett, C. K. *The Gospel According to St. John: An Introduction with Commentary and Notes on the Greek Text.* Second Edition. Philadelphia: The Westminster Press, 1978.

Bava Kamma, see Schorr, *Talmud Bavli.*

Bav. Bat., Bava Batra, see Schorr, *Talmud Bavli.*

Bav. Metzia, see Schorr, *Talmud Bavli.*

B. B., Bava Basra, see Schorr, *Talmud Bavli.*

Beasley-Murray, George R. In David R. Hubbard and Glen W. Barker (Gen. Eds.), *Word Biblical Commentary.* Volume 36. *John.* Waco, TX: Word Books, 1987.

Ben-Abba, Dov. *Signet Hebrew-English English-Hebrew Dictionary.* Massada-Press/Modan Publishing House Ltd., Israel, 1977.

Ben Avraham, Rabbi Alexander, and Sharfman, Rabbi Benjamin (Eds.). *The Pentateuch and Rashi's Commentary.* Brooklyn, NY: S. S. & R. Publishing Company, Inc. (also Philadelphia: Press of the Jewish Publication Society), 1976.

Bent, A. C., see Christensen.

Ber., Berachot, see Schorr, *Talmud Bavli*.

Birnbaum, Philip. *Encyclopedia of Jewish Concepts*. NY: Hebrew
Publishing Company, 1993.

Birnbaum, Philip (Ed.). *Maimonides' Mishneh Torah*. New York:
Hebrew Publishing Co., 1985.

Blackman, Philip (Ed.). *Mishnayoth*. Gateshead: Judaica Press,
Ltd., 1983.

The Book of Legends: Sefer Ha-Aggadah. Bialik, Hayim N. and
Ravnitzky, Yehoshua H. (Eds.). New York: Schocken, 1992.

Brown, Raymond E. *The Gospel According to John. The Anchor
Bible*. Volumes 29, 29A. Garden City, NY: Doubleday and
Company, Inc., 1984.

Bruce, F. F. *The Epistle to the Hebrews*. In F. F. Bruce (Gen. Ed.),
The New International Commentary on the New Testament.
Grand Rapids, MI: Wm. B. Eerdmans, 1979.

Bullinger, E. W. *Figures of Speech Used in the Bible*. Grand Rapids,
MI: Baker Book House, 1987. (Original work publ. in 1898).

Carson, D. A. *Exegetical Fallacies*. Grand Rapids, MI, Baker Book
House, 1984.

Carson, D. A. *Matthew*. In Frank E. Gaebelein (Gen. Ed.), *The
Expositor's Bible Commentary*. Volume 8. Grand Rapids, MI:
Zondervan, 1984.

Childs, Brevard S. *Biblical Theology of the Old and New Testaments:
Theological Reflection on the Christian Bible*. Minneapolis:
Fortress Press, 1993.

Christensen, Duane L. In Bruce M. Metzger (Gen. Ed.), *Word
Biblical Commentary*. Volume 6A. *Deuteronomy 1:1–21:9*. Second
Edition. Waco, TX: Word Books, 2001.

Christensen, Duane L. In Bruce M. Metzger (Gen. Ed.), *Word
Biblical Commentary*. Volume 6B. *Deuteronomy 21:10–34:12*.
Waco, TX: Word Books, 2002.

Chul., Chulin, see Schorr, *Talmud Bavli*.

Cohen, A. (Gen. Ed.). *Soncino Books of the Bible*. Volumes 1–14.
London: The Soncino Press Limited, 1978.

Concordance to the Novum Testamentum Graece. Third edition. Berlin: Walter De Gruyter, 1987.

Dauermann, Stuart. "Great and Wonderful." in Jews for Jesus (Ed.) *Avodat Y'shua*. San Francisco: Purple Pomegranate, 1991.

Drazin, Israel. *Targum Onkelos to Deuteronomy: an English Translation of the Text with Analysis and Commentary* (Based on the A. Sperber Edition). Ktav Publishing House, Inc., 1982.

Driver, S. R. *The International Critical Commentary: Deuteronomy*. Edinburgh: T&T Clark, 1996.

Driver, S. R., Plummer, A., and Briggs, C. A. (Gen. Eds.). *The International Critical Commentary on the Holy Scriptures of the Old and New Testaments*. Edinburgh: T. & T. Clark, 1979. (Original work published 1896–1924).

Ellingworth, Paul. *The Epistle to the Hebrews*. In I. Howard Marshall and W. Ward Gasque (Gen. Eds.), *The New International Greek New Testament Commentary*. Grand Rapids, MI: William B. Eerdmans Publishing Company, 1993.

Elwell, W. A. (Ed.). *Evangelical Dictionary of Theology*. Grand Rapids, MI: Baker Book House, 1984.

Evans, Louis H., Jr. *Hebrews*. In Lloyd J. Ogilvie (Gen. Ed.), *The Communicator's Commentary*. Dallas: Word Publishing, 1985.

Even-Shoshan, Avraham (Ed.). *New Concordance for the Torah, Prophets, and Writings*. Jerusalem: Sivan Press, 1977.

Faulkner, Raymond O. *A Concise Dictionary of Middle Egyptian*. Griffith Institute, Oxford: University Press, 1999.

Feinberg, Jeffrey Enoch. *Walk Exodus!* Baltimore: Messianic Jewish Publishers, 1999.

Feinberg, Jeffrey Enoch. *Walk Genesis!* Baltimore: Messianic Jewish Publishers, 1998.

Feinberg, Jeffrey Enoch. *Walk Leviticus!* Baltimore: Messianic Jewish Publishers, 2001.

Feinberg, Jeffrey Enoch. *Walk Numbers!* Baltimore: Messianic Jewish Publishers, 2002.

Feinberg, Pat. *Jot & Tittle*. Littleton, CO: First Fruits of Zion, 1998.

Feinberg, Pat. *Search the Sidra*. Littleton, CO: First Fruits of Zion,

2001.

Fisch, S. *Ezekiel*. In A. Cohen (Gen. Ed.), *The Soncino Books of the Bible*. Volume 7. London: The Soncino Press, Ltd., 1978.

Fishbane, Michael. *Haftarot*. In Nahum M. Sarna (Gen. Ed.), *The JPS Bible Commentary*. Philadelphia: Jewish Publication Society, 2002.

Fox, Everett. *The Schocken Bible: The Five Books of Moses*. Volume 1. New York: Schocken Books, 1995.

Frankel, Ellen and Teutsch, Betsy P. (1992). *The Encyclopedia of Jewish Symbols*. Northvale, NJ: Jason Aronson, 1992.

Friedman, Rabbi Alexander Zusia. *Wellsprings of Torah*. Transl. by Gertrude Hirschler. New York: Judaica Press, Inc., 1990.

Gellis, Maurice and Gribetz, Dennis. *The Glory of Torah Reading*. Revised edition. Monsey, NY: M.P. Press, Inc., 1996.

Gen.R., Genesis Rabbah, see *The Soncino Midrash Rabbah*.

Ginzberg, Louis. *The Legends of the Jews*. Volume 2. Transl. by Henrietta Szold. Baltimore: The Johns Hopkins University Press, 1998.

Gundry, Robert H. *Matthew: A Commentary on his Literary and Theological Art*. Grand Rapids, MI: Wm. B. Eerdmans Publishing Company, 1982.

Hays, Richard B. *Echoes of Scripture in the Letters of Paul*. New Haven: Yale University Press, 1989.

Herczeg, Rabbi Yisra'el Isser Zvi (Ed.). *The Torah: With Rashi's Commentary Translated, Annotated, and Elucidated*. Artscroll Series/The Sapirstein Edition. Brooklyn: Mesorah Publications, Ltd., 1995.

Hertz, Dr. J. H. (Ed.). *The Pentateuch and Haftorahs*. Second edition. London: Soncino Press, 1975.

Heschel, Abraham J. *The Prophets*. Volume 1. NY: Harper and Row, Publishers, 1969.

Hil. Teph., Hilchot Tefillin, see Rambam, Birnbaum (Ed.), *Maimonides' Mishneh Torah*.

Hilton, Rabbi Michael and Marshall, Fr. Gordion. *The Gospels & Rabbinic Judaism: A Study Guide*. Hoboken, NJ: KTAV, 1988.

Hirsch, Samson Raphael, Trans. *The Pentateuch, Haftarah, and the Five Megillot.* Ed. by Ephraim Oratz. New York: The Judaica Press, Inc., 1990. (English translation by Gertrude Hirschler; German work published in 1867–1878).

Ibn Ezra, see Schorr, *Talmud Bavli.*

ibn Paquda, R. Bachya. *Duties of the Heart.* Transl. by Moses Hyamson. Jerusalem: Feldheim Publishers, 1986. (Translated from Arabic into Hebrew by R. Yehuda Ibn Tibbon).

JPS, Jewish Publication Society, see *Tanakh: The Holy Scriptures.*

Kahan, Rabbi Aharon. *The Taryag Mitzvos.* Brooklyn: Keser Torah Pub., 1988. (Based on the classical *Sefer haChinuch*).

Kantor, Mattis. *The Jewish Time Line Encyclopedia: A Year-by-Year History from Creation to the Present.* Northvale, NJ: Jason Aronson, Inc., 1989.

Keil, C. F. and Delitzsch, F. *Commentary on the Old Testament.* Transl. by James Martin. Volumes 1–10. Grand Rapids, MI: William B. Eerdmans Publishing Company, 1976.

Kestenbaum Edition, see *Tikkun: The Torah Reader's Compendium.*

Kohlenberger, John R. III (Ed.). *The NIV Interlinear Hebrew-English Old Testament.* Grand Rapids, MI: Zondervan Publishing House, 1979.

Kolatch, Alfred J. *The Complete Dictionary of English and Hebrew First Names.* Middle Village, NY: Jonathan David Publishers, Inc., 1984.

Lachs, Samuel Tobias. *A Rabbinic Commentary on the New Testament.* Hoboken, NJ: KTAV Publishing House, Inc., 1987.

Lane, William L. *Hebrews: A Call to Commitment.* Peabody, MA: Hendrickson Publishers, 1988.

Lane, William L. *Word Biblical Commentary: Hebrews 1–13.* Volumes 47a, 47b. Waco, TX: Word Books, Publisher, 1991.

Legends, see *The Book of Legends.*

Leibowitz, Nehama. *Studies in Devarim (Deuteronomy).* Transl. by Aryeh Newman. Revised ed. Jerusalem: Hemed Press, 1986.

Longenecker, Richard N. *Acts.* In Frank E. Gaebelein (Gen. Ed.). *The Expositor's Bible Commentary.* Vol. 9. Grand Rapids:

Zondervan, 1981.

M. Chul., Mishnah Chullin, see Blackman, *Mishnayoth*.

Meg., Megillah, see Schorr, *Talmud Bavli*.

Mekhilta According to Rabbi Ishmael: An Analytical Translation. Transl. by Jacob Neusner. Volume 1. Atlanta: Scholars Press, Brown Judaic Studies, 1988.

The Metsudah Pirkei Avos: The Wisdom of the Fathers. Selected and translated by Rabbi Avrohom Davis. New York: Metsudah Publications, 1986.

Midrash Tanchuma. See Townsend, John T.

MK, Moed Kattan, see Schorr, *Talmud Bavli*.

Morris, Leon. *The Gospel According to John.* In F. F. Bruce (Gen. Ed.), *The New International Commentary on the New Testament.* Grand Rapids, MI: Wm B. Eerdmans Publ. Co., 1979.

Mounce, Robert H. *The Book of Revelation.* In F. F. Bruce (Gen. Ed.), *The New International Commentary on the New Testament.* Grand Rapids, MI: Wm B. Eerdmans Publ. Co., 1977.

M. Pe'ah, Mishnah Pe'ah, see Blackman, *Mishnayoth*.

M. Sukk., Mishnah Sukkot, see Blackman, *Mishnayoth*.

Munk, Rabbi Elie. *The Call of the Torah: An Anthology of Interpretation and Commentary on the Five Books of Moses: Devarim.* Translated from the French by E. S. Mazer. Edited by Yitzchok Kirzner. In R. Nosson Scherman and R. Meir Zlotowitz (Eds.), *ArtScroll Mesorah Series.* Brooklyn, NY: Mesorah Publications, Ltd., 1995.

Nachshoni, Yehuda. *Studies in the Weekly Parashah.* Transl. by Shmuel Himelstein. Volume 5: Devarim. Brooklyn: Mesorah Publications, Ltd., 1989.

NAV, see ORT.

Ned., Nedarim, see Schorr, *Talmud Bavli*.

Neusner, Jacob. *Sifre to Deuteronomy: an Analytical Translation.* Volume 1, Pisqaot One through One Hundred Forty-Three. Brown Judaic Studies 98. Atlanta: Scholars Press, 1987.

The New English Bible. Standard edition. New York: Oxford University Press, 1971.

Novum Testamentum Graece. Nestle-Aland Edition. Stuttgart: Deutsche Bibelstiftung, 1981.

Onkelos, Targum Onkelos, see Drazin, Israel.

Oppen, Menachem Moshe. *The Yom Kippur Avodah.* The Pictorial Avodah Series. C.I. S. Distributors. Baltimore: M'chon Harbotzas Torah, Inc., Chicago: Chicago Community Kollel, 1988.

ORT, *Navigating the Bible: Interactive Bar/Bat Mitzvah CD-Rom.* Sung by Cantor Moshe Haschel. London: World ORT Union, 1998.

Plaut, W. Gunther and Bamberger, Bernard J. *The Torah: A Modern Commentary.* New York: UAHC Press, 1981.

Plaut, W. G. and Stern, Chaim. *The Haftarah Commentary.* New York: UAHC Press, 1996.

Radak, Rabbi David Kimchi. See Schorr, *Talmud Bavli.*

Rambam, see Birnbaum, *Maimonides' Mishneh Torah.*

Ramban (Nachmanides), *Commentary on the Torah: Deuteronomy.* Transl. by Rabbi Dr. Charles B. Chavel. New York: Shilo Publishing House, 1976.

Rashi. See Ben Avraham, Rabbi Abraham et al. or Herczek, Rabbi Yisra'el Isser Zvi.

R.H., Rosh HaShannah, see Schorr, *Talmud Bavli.*

Robertson, A. T. *Word Pictures in the New Testament.* Grand Rapids, MI: Baker Book House, 1932.

Sailhamer, John H. *The Pentateuch as Narrative.* Grand Rapids, MI: Zondervan Publishing House, 1992.

Sanders, Paul. *Provenance of Deuteronomy 32.* Leiden: E.J. Brill, 1996.

Sanh., Sanhedrin, see Schorr, *Talmud Bavli.*

Scherman, Rabbi Nosson (Gen. Ed.). *The Chumash: The Torah, Haftaros, and Five Megillos with a Commentary Anthologized from the Rabbinic Writings.* Ed. by Rabbi Hersh Goldwurn, Rabbi Avie Gold, and Rabbi Meir Zlotowitz. Artscroll Series, The Stone Edition. Brooklyn: Mesorah Publications, Ltd., 1995.

Schorr, Rabbi Yisroel Simcha (Gen. Ed.). *Talmud Bavli.* The Artscroll Series, Schottenstein Edition. Brooklyn: Mesorah Publications, Ltd., 1993.

Sed. Olam, *Seder Olam: The Rabbinic View of Biblical Chronology.*
Transl. by Heinrich W. Guggenheimer. Northvale, NJ: Jason
Aronson Inc., 1998.

Sforno, Ovadiah. *Commentary on the Torah.* Transl. by Rabbi
Raphael Pelcovitz. The Artscroll Mesorah Series. Brooklyn:
Mesorah Publications, Ltd., 1997.

Shabb., Shabbos, see Schorr, *Talmud Bavli.*

Shev., Shevuos, see Schorr, *Talmud Bavli.*

Shulman, Eliezer. *The Sequence of Events in the Old Testament.*
Transl. by Sarah Lederhendler. Fifth edition. Jerusalem: Bank
Hapoalim and Ministry of Defense—Publishing House, 1987.

Sifre, Sifrei, see Neusner, Jacob.

Soncino, see A. Cohen (Ed.), *The Soncino Books of the Bible.*

The Soncino Midrash Rabbah. The CD Rom Judaic Classics
Library. Distributed by Davka Corporation. Brooklyn, NY:
Soncino Press, 1983.

Sot., Sotah, see Schorr, *Talmud Bavli.*

Stern, David H., Trans. *Complete Jewish Bible.* Clarksville, MD:
Jewish New Testament Publications, 1998.

Stern, David H. *Jewish New Testament Commentary.* Clarksville,
MD: Jewish New Testament Publications, 1992.

Stone Edition, see Scherman, Rabbi Nosson (Gen. Ed.).

Sukk., Sukkot, see Schorr, *Talmud Bavli.*

Taan., Taanis, see Schorr, *Talmud Bavli.*

Talmud, see Schorr, *Talmud Bavli.*

Tanakh: The Holy Scriptures. Philadelphia: Jewish Publication
Society, 1988.

Tanch., Tanchuma or Tanhuma, see Townsend, *Midrash Tanhuma.*

TDOT, see *Theological Dictionary of the Old Testament.*

Tenney, Merrill C. *John.* In Frank E. Gaebelein (Gen. Ed.), *The
Expositor's Bible Commentary.* Volume 9. Grand Rapids, MI:
Zondervan, 1981.

Ter., Terumoth, see Blackman, *Mishnayoth.*

Theological Dictionary of the Old Testament. Botterweck, G. J. and
Ringgren, H. (Gen. Eds.). Grand Rapids, MI: William B.

Eerdmans Publishing Co., 1975.

Tigay, Jeffrey H. *Deuteronomy.* In Nahum M. Sarna (Gen. Ed.), *The JPS Torah Commentary.* Philadelphia: The Jewish Publication Society, 1996.

Tikkun Kor'im haM'fuar. Brooklyn, NY: Im haSefer, 1994.

Tikkun: The Torah Reader's Compendium. Chumash commentary by Rabbi Avie Gold. Artscroll Series, the Kestenbaum Edition. Brooklyn, NY: Mesorah Publications, Ltd., 2002.

Townsend, John T. *Midrash Tanhuma.* Translated into English with Indices and Brief Notes (S. Buber Recension). Hoboken, NY: KTAV Publishing House, 1997.

T.Y. Meg., Talmud Yerushalmi Megillah, in Kestenbaum, p. 488.

Unger, Merrill F. (Ed.). *Unger's Bible Dictionary.* Chicago: Moody Press, 1979.

Walk Genesis/Exodus/Leviticus/Numbers!, see Feinberg.

Werblowsky, Dr. R. J. Zwi and Wigoder, Dr. Geoffrey (Eds.). *The Encyclopedia of the Jewish Religion.* Jerusalem: Masada, 1967.

Wigoder, Geoffrey (Gen. Ed.). "Hakhel" in *Encyclopedia of Judaism.* New York: Macmillan Publishing Co., 1989.

Wigram, George V. *The Englishman's Hebrew and Chaldee Concordance of the Old Testament.* Grand Rapids, MI: Baker Book House, 1980. (Original work published in 1843).

The Works of Josephus. Transl. by William Whiston. Lynn, MA: Hendrickson Publishers, 1980.

Wright, Christopher. *Deuteronomy.* In Robert L. Hubbard Jr. and Robert K. Johnson (O.T. Eds.), *New International Biblical Commentary.* Volume 4. Peabody, MA: Hendrickson Pub., 1996.

Yad Chazakah, see Birnbaum, *Maimonides' Mishneh Torah.*

Yad, Ned., Nedarim, see Birnbaum, *Maimonides' Mishneh Torah.*

Yad, Par. Adum., Parah Adumah, see Birnbaum, *Maimonides' Mishneh Torah.*

Yad, Sanh., Sanhedrin, see Birnbaum, *Maimonides' Mishneh Torah.*

Yev., Yevamoth, see Schorr, *Talmud Bavli.*

Yoma, see Schorr, *Talmud Bavli.*

Zav., Zavim, see Blackman, *Mishnayoth.*